Astrology and Vocational Aptitude

H. Baron von Klockler

ISBN-10: 0-86690-166-3
ISBN-13: 978-0-86690-166-6

Cover Design: Jack Cipolla

Published by:
American Federation of Astrologers, Inc.
6535 S. Rural Road
Tempe, AZ 85283

www.astrologers.com

Printed in the United States of America

Translator's Preface

The greatest difficulties the student of astrology faces are to be found in the area of horoscope *interpretation*—combining, with some coherent and organized significance, all those random and separate factors which he has learned have particular meanings, but which when viewed together appear confusing and frequently contradictory so that the student is left at a loss as to how to proceed. While there are many good textbooks where the basic principles of astrology are adequately set forth, there are few astrologers who have published works specifically on the *integration* of the horoscope into a comprehensive, holistic pattern that are simple, systematic, and useful, as well as unencumbered by dubious speculations.

Not much is known about the life of Herbert von Klockler, except that he was at the center of a prestigious group of intellectuals and astrologers in Leipzig during the brief but brilliant renaissance of astrology in Germany following the First World War. The intellectual climate of modern Germany has always been favorable for the study of subjects such as astrology, and the impact of modern psychology in the German-speaking countries resulted in an extensive critical reevaluation of astrological tradition and its methods. The author's book *Principles of Astrological Interpretation*, which was published in 1926, reflected this new approach or evaluation, and placed him among the foremost astrological writers in the Europe of that day. The present work is short, but is nevertheless an application of those principles to the area of vocational aptitude—an area in which the author always maintained a special interest. Considerable research and thought went into it.

A member of an old aristocratic family, von Klockler eventually became a physician but by the late 1930s had ceased all of his astrological activities; apparently he saw the handwriting on the wall when many of his astrological colleagues were arrested and imprisoned by the Nazis. In any case, this brilliant period had come to an untimely close. Von Klockler himself escaped arrest as he occupied his time with the treatment and rehabilitation of German veterans and casualties and abandoned—at least outwardly—all his former interest in astrology. He died in 1950 at age 53.

My experience in teaching astrology has been that the student feels overwhelmed by the diversity and complexity of the many astrological factors he feels he must handle all at the same time. For this reason the present work will be of inestimable value since the author's purpose is always to simplify and streamline the principles of interpretation, and even to eliminate many traditional factors—the "witches-kettle" of which he speaks in his introductory remarks that may at first shock the student. No matter. It is better to have a simplified but coherent system with which to begin, and then later, after having acquired more experience, the student can experiment for himself with those rulers, parts, mathematical points, sensitive degrees, etc., and form his own opinion of them. But it is important to be able to see the breadth of the forest before one begins to examine the individual trees, and herein lies the value for the student of von Klockler's system of interpretation.

Contents

FOREWORD

This book has been written—strange to say—for practical-use. A large number of persons interested in astrology assisted in the collection of the basic data and thanks to their help and advice it has been possible to put together a fairly comprehensive study. To those who so willingly gave me their assistance, I feel obliged to make accessible as soon as possible my interpretations of the complete material, and as their interests lie primarily, and quite understandably, in the practical interpretation of the horoscope it becomes my duty, and my pleasure as well, to help these laymen by showing them more valid methods of horoscope interpretation. Even a glance at contemporary astrological literature will immediately show how drastic has become the need for more valid principles of interpretation, as well as the need for a sense of *limitation,* since the unrestrained fantasy usually found in present-day horoscope interpretation is of no value whatsoever. Furthermore, many people whose interest in astrology is superficial seem quite unwilling even to attempt to interpret the horoscope within the limits of individual psychology. As long as there is no systematic research in the field of astrology, and no likelihood of establishing an organization for this purpose, the mistakes that will continue to be made in the practical interpretation of the horoscope are quite inevitable, although any serious attempt to bring them to light and deal with them has the value of making the student aware of at least some of the mistakes of the past.

In *Astrology as an Empirical Science* I discussed in brief some of the material included in this book. However, since that time, considerable new material has been made available to me, and I felt I wanted to present in greater detail the observations and conclusions I had reached regarding the use of astrology in determining the most suitable vocation or life-work. The conclusions given here are only part of what I hope may in the future be an even larger and more comprehensive work, but even as given here the reader will find guidelines for more valid horoscope interpretation and, I hope, stimulus for further research.

I find that in consideration of the whole problem, one main difficulty is that the motives that underlay an inclination to a particular vocation are not always clear. Astrology can frequently provide an understanding of the psychology underlying the interest shown in any vocation, and I have tested my findings with doctors and teachers and others and feel they are quite trustworthy. In many cases sheer talent provides the reason for interest in a particular vocation, while in other cases psychological conflicts provide the motive for such an interest. It is not really the fault of astrology that these things are not as clear as they might be, for the literature of modern psychology has almost nothing to say on the subject of vocational motivation.

The student is recommended to compare at all times the sample horoscopes with the commentary in the text. By looking at the horoscope, the student will obtain a clearer picture than any amount of reading can provide. I do not feel that the problem is one of learning to combine the various separate astrological factors; it seems to me that these days rather too much than too little is put to combination, and in all this activity the fundamental message of the horoscope is often overlooked. The problem is one of *learning to see.* A horoscope that is correctly *seen* has already been interpreted. The correct way to *see* the horoscope is at first to disregard the succedent and cadent houses and only to consider the relation of the planets to the angular cusps, and to the hemispheres and quadrants of the horoscope. In this way one gradually comes to feel that the Placidus system of house division is quite inadequate and, for the advanced student, dispensable. One discovers that the Placidus concept of twelve distinctly separate houses is not as practicable as a simple division of the four quadrants into three equal parts—as was suggested by Porphyry, Flambart, and Grimm. Although this system of equal house division seems to me to work out better, I have adhered to the Placidus system in the example horoscopes given in this book, as that system is the one with which the reader is most likely to be familiar.

As much as possible, the horoscopes considered in the text are of famous individuals, as these provide the most vivid and striking examples of the talents and abilities required in the vocations discussed, and the most convincing illustration of principles. Many of these cases will demonstrate important new points in astrological interpretation that have never before been brought out.

No acknowledgment of other astrological works is necessary here. Whenever I wished to refer to some point of traditional astrological interpretation in order to weigh its justifiability, I have consulted Brandler-Pracht's *Prognose* to see whether or not I could agree. I also wish to mention the authors Claudius Ptolemy, Strauch-Leovitius, and Abdias Trew. The elementary principles which underlay the present work have been explained in the chapter "Order of Horoscope Factors" in my *Principles of Astrological Interpretation*.

The members of the Leipzig Astrological Society have helped immeasurably in contributing much of the material, and in doing so greatly facilitated my work. I wish to give special thanks to my wife Gertrude as well as Miss E. Lohnert.

H. Baron von Klockler

INTRODUCTION

For many men and women the choice of a suitable vocation is a major issue in their lives, and subsequent success or failure in the vocation determines to a large extent their entire outlook on life. It is said that the desire for power is basic to human nature, and if it is so it is in the vocation or life-work that this desire finds its most civilized expression. But success is assured only when the individual shows innate capacity for his vocation as well as the ability to cooperate, if need be, with others in the same work.

Psychology and various forms of character analysis are now concerned with finding ways to evaluate personality with an eye to assisting the individual in choosing the most suitable vocation.

Graphology and physiognomy, despite their value at other times, have not shown themselves able to demonstrate valid conclusions in the matter of vocational guidance. Either their basic principles and areas of best application seem unsuitable for this particular purpose, or as sciences they are not sufficiently developed at the present time. At their present stage of development, graphology and physiognomy cannot be used to determine the existence of personality traits and inclinations that would enable one to go on to conclude that a specific vocation would or would not be appropriate.

So-called industrial psychology, which came into vogue several years ago, has also been unable to show that it can produce anything very useful. Its methods are not subtle enough to determine ability for more intellectual vocations, and it can be used with profit only for the determination of a suitable trade or craft. Then too, all methods that utilize *examinations* are beset by difficulties. It frequently turns out that those who have done well on examinations later do not fulfill expectations, while those who do poorly on examinations encounter no difficulty later on. An examination, no matter how skillfully it has been prepared, cannot eliminate those mistakes resulting from an indisposition or difficulty that may be quite temporary, or may even recur periodically. It is true that progress in the study of industrial psychology is complicated by both social and economic difficulties, and that under better conditions it might be able to accomplish much more.

An examination places the examinee under a pressure that may easily prevent him from demonstrating all he is capable of doing, and we have noted that certain other character traits, which in a brief and impersonal examination can be neither discovered nor evaluated, may later help overcome initial problems or insecurities. Dr. Alfred Adler, in a lecture in Dresden, expressed this idea when he said, perhaps with some exaggeration, that the very lack of a specific talent or ability can be for certain persons a strong incentive to achievement, as it was for Demosthenes and apparently many others in history.

In addition to the indication of vocational capabilities, there are traits of character and social adjustment to be taken into consideration, but these are much more difficult to incorporate into an objective examination. To some extent the psychology of Freud and Adler has established the principles on which a judgment with respect to an individual's inner life can be made, and they have clarified the dynamics and development of certain instinctual drives; but their methods are not suitable for an evaluation of vocational ability as they are far too oriented toward psychopathology.

The fact is there is no method in modern psychology that gives a complete, or even nearly complete, evaluation of the personality *as a whole*, while astrology—as a serious scientific discipline—is able to do so with some validity. This should not seem strange, as astrologers have for centuries been consulted on questions of career, and in a sense it has always been astrology's purpose to determine vocational aptitude from the horoscope.

In days when society's economic and social structure was more simple, and the number and kinds of professions were more limited, it may well have been possible to make an adequate evaluation of the horoscope by using relatively simple rules and formulas. But a complex society and the diverse needs of modern civilization, with the consequent increase in the variety of vocational possibilities, require the astrologer to establish newer and more comprehensive principles for evaluating vocational aptitude. Modern astrology, based on the best of astrological tradition, the more important discoveries of modern psychology and psychoanalysis, can provide reliable guidelines. Of course, astrology cannot be used to resolve every problem that may arise in evaluating vocational aptitude, but it seems capable of presenting a good overall picture that is at the same time reliable, and this is particularly true when the client is not unwilling to assist the astrologer by supplying information on his environment, realistic possibilities, etc. As in many other areas, astrology's use here is as an invaluable auxiliary, but considered as some kind of oracle, it must often fail, and even then largely because the number of really talented astrologers is very small. Anyway, such arbitrary predictions are not to the point in a work of this sort.

In this book I have attempted to lay down some principles of interpretation that differ somewhat from the traditional approach. In the matter of vocational guidance I consider it impossible to make a satisfactory interpretation on the basis of any single planet and its position. There is really no such thing as a "Saturn vocation," or a "Jupiter vocation" or a "Mars vocation," although, for example, astrological tradition states that Mars rules butchers, doctors, soldiers, smiths, etc. But the length of this list, even as it is, shows that *specific* judgments cannot be obtained in this way. Of course, Mars plays a role in these professions, but always as part of a larger configuration, and this configuration is the important thing. Besides, we know that a Mars component is important or even necessary in other vocational areas, and traditional astrology has little to say about this. Of what value then is the concept of a Mars vocation?

I also think that the sign on the Midheaven is of no significance because it is other placements in the horoscope that actually condition vocational aptitude. Certainly, the tenth, second, and perhaps also the sixth house, have generalized meanings that are applicable to the vocation, but for determining the vocation itself these houses are important only when they contain planets that are strongly placed. Instead, the signs on the tenth, second, and sixth houses indicate the individual manner in which the profession is pursued—a sort of functional rhythm of the individual in this regard. Moreover, given the circumstances, any of the houses can assume significance in connection with the vocation, but no single factor can be decisive by itself; one must study the whole horoscope as well as the whole person.

In the following pages the reader will notice that the so-called house rulers are not taken into consideration. The unbiased examination of a great many horoscopes shows without question that their use cannot be taken seriously. For example, during the approximately two hours that a sign passes over the Midheaven, the ruler of the tenth house remains the same, and for that reason cannot have enough individualized significance to be considered as dominant and therefore able to influence vocational aptitude. Also, the planetary ruler of any given cusp may remain for days, weeks, or even months in the same sign. And finally, it goes without saying that I disregard the whole witches' kettle of dispositors, decanate rulers, antiscions, mundane horoscopes, etc.

What seem to me to be artificial and unnecessary complications have been left out and only the relative strength of the planets in relation to the angular houses has been taken into consideration. The attentive reader will see that much greater clarity is obtained and a more reliable evaluation of vocational aptitudes can be made.

The nature of the various professions is discussed first, and an attempt is then made to establish what must be the corresponding astrological factors. These factors are not presented in rules, formulas or schematic form, as such rules, though they may have a certain limited value, cannot be solely relied upon.

Preliminary Remarks

Personality Types

With respect to vocational aptitude, five types of individuals can be distinguished, and they must be approached differently in any vocational guidance consultation.

1. A pronounced and unmistakable talent in one specific direction. Here, an evaluation is easy to make as the horoscope indications are striking and clear.

2. A versatile personality with several talents, but with the resulting tendency to frequent changes in the profession. Advice is difficult because there is interest and ability for several vocations, which can be seen in the horoscope. But there is no continual urge toward one specific vocation, and the horoscope should mirror this problem. In more favorable instances, the individual's character and ingenuity may be such that he can create a line of work that will encompass all or most of his capabilities. The astrologer will have to use all his art to assist in finding such an unusual or original line of work.

3. The vocation is not a focal point of interest. Instead, personal, family, or other concerns are the main source of pleasure or disappointment in life. Advice on a suitable profession can be given only when specific abilities for one vocation are clearly shown.

4. There is a general lack of any ability at all. It is best to proceed by excluding all vocations that are clearly impossible for the individual, and then to consider whatever is left. But after all, one cannot come up with some specialized field of work for an unskilled worker who seems likely to remain so.

5. Illness or psychopathology preclude the serious pursuit of any profession. The horoscope will adequately reflect any such unfortunate conditions.

It is necessary first of all to establish to which of these five classifications the horoscope under consideration belongs. Most cases fall into groups two to five, and it seems to be a common situation that the astrologer is approached by parents who wish to learn of any marked ability or possible talent that their young children may possess.

The evaluation of the cases in the first group is easy, and the wise application of even the simple formulas of astrological tradition will lead to correct conclusions. In the other four groups these traditional formulas are practically useless. Even in group one their uncritical use may enable one to determine the specific vocation which is most suitable, but the finer details, which may vary considerably, cannot be determined. But it is precisely in the appreciation of detail that lies the real value of the method of interpretation given here.

Dominance and Structure: the Basic Elements of Horoscope Delineation

It should always be remembered that the cases are rare wherein a single, isolated talent alone determines what the vocation will be. More frequently, several abilities will be found together in a combination that points to some particular vocation. In addition to this, other general character traits can be equally decisive in determining whether there will be a successful adjustment in the vocation.

In every case then, all traits of the personality are significant and a thorough consideration of the horoscope as a whole is always advisable. The essentials of horoscope delineation are not within the scope of the present work, but the method outlined here proceeds from an evaluation of the *dominant* horoscope factors, and their relative importance compared to those factors which are not dominant.

These dominant factors in the horoscope are always of the greatest importance in determining vocational capacity. Usually, several dominant horoscope factors are found in that group of persons having many and varied talents who are suitable for several professions. Too few and too weakly placed factors of dominance are characteristic of group four—those individuals lacking in ability.

These dominant factors do not *by themselves* determine whatever ability there may be, but in fact are conditioned to a certain extent by the general structure of the horoscope. The problem of structure is a problem that today is all too seldom discussed. F. Glahn has made some interesting observations on this subject, but his interpretations were too specific and concrete, and would be valid only in the most self-evident situations. A few remarks on the subject are therefore in order here.

The overall structure of the horoscope results from the distribution therein of the various planets and signs. The general pattern for a given twenty-four hour period will be called the *general* structure; this results from the positions of the planets in the zodiacal signs and from their mutual aspects. Astrological tradition is rich in the number of aphorisms meant to clarify the meaning of these positions, but as they are always an interpretation of isolated factors they cannot be used alone in the judgment of *overall* general structure. *Individual* structure results from the particu- larization of general structure that takes place when the time of birth is also considered. It includes the relationship of the zodiacal signs to the angular houses, the position of the planets within the houses and their aspects to the angular cusps; it is this last possibility that results in a planet's dominance. The dominant factors form a part of the structure; although they are not the structure itself, they are the most important part of that structure. Individualization of the personality is determined by the *birth time* and the number and strength of dominant factors that particular time of birth makes possible.

An understanding of the structural features of a horoscope is not always simple, but ideally one should be able to grasp at a glance the combined effects of quite diverse factors. A knowledge of the various structural types underlies this understanding. The classifications given here are quite general and, of course, are always subject to modification by other important elements.

I. General structure types.

a. The spring signs—expansive and active.

b. The summer signs—same as the spring signs but less so.

c. The autumn signs—balance between expansive and intensive.

d. The winter signs—predominantly intensive.

e. Planets in conjunction or close groupings—usually indicates a one-sidedness of the personality according to the nature of the planets and signs involved.

f. Planets distributed throughout the horoscope—indicates versatility, and a possible balancing out of forces; an even, uniform, and all around development is favored.

g. The opposition—strongly polarized tendencies, often with creative ability.

h. The square—indicates inhibition, inability, or restriction.

i. The trine—the natures of the planets function harmoniously.

j. The sextile—same as the trine, but with an active-passive polarization due to the difference in triplicity of the signs involved.

k. The triplicities—these are traditionally described as fire, earth, air, and water (three signs in each group).

l. The quadruplicities—these are traditionally described as cardinal, fixed, and mutable or common (four signs in each group).

II. Individual structure types. There is often a similarity to the general structure types.

a. East type—the planets are mainly in the eastern half of the horoscope. The Midheaven-IC axis can be regarded as the axis of emotional and physical reaction. The eastern half is expansive and active emotionally and physically.

b. West type—the planets are mainly in the western half of the horoscope. This type is more passive or receptive in emotional and physical reactions. The horizon is the axis of mental or intellectual, and possibly spiritual, response.

c. Day type—the planets are mainly above the horizon, indicating an active and outgoing mentality; objectivity.

d. Night type—the planets are mainly below the horizon, indicating a passive or receptive mentality; subjectivity.

The following sub-types appear when east-west hemispheres are combined with day-night hemispheres.

1. The first quadrant (first, second, and third houses) combines the night with the east and is passive mentally, but active emotionally and physically.

2. The second quadrant (fourth, fifth, and sixth houses) combines the night with the west and is receptive mentally, emotionally, and physically.

3. The third. quadrant (seventh, eighth, and ninth houses) combines the west with the day and therefore is emotionally and physically receptive but mentally active and outgoing.

4. The fourth quadrant (tenth, eleventh, and twelfth houses) combines the east with the day and is outgoing and active emotionally, physically as well as mentally; this is the strongest quadrant of the horoscope.

Both the nature of certain basic drives and their rate of development can be seen by studying the quadrants. It is only natural that the emotionally passive west type will develop more slowly than the active and expansive east type, which, because of its nature, comes into conflict with the environment at a younger age and develops more rapidly as a result.

e. Angular house type—a predominance of planets in angular houses inclines to greater activity. In this respect the first and tenth houses are stronger than the fourth and seventh for the reasons made clear above. The fourth and seventh houses transfer this action to more personal, introverted. or subjective pursuits.

f. Succedent house type—the planets are placed predominantly in the second, fifth, eighth, and eleventh houses; there is more stability but less activity than in the angular house type (compare the nature of the fixed signs).

g. Cadent house type—a predominance of planets in the third, sixth, ninth, and twelfth houses; this is active but changeable, and the sphere of activity is mental. However, a judgment on the quality of intelligence cannot be made from an analysis of the structural type, but such a judgment may be possible from an analysis of the dominant factors.

Finally, several planets in a house form a particular structural element, the meaning of which can be found in any good textbook.

In most cases, a given horoscope is a combination of several types of general and individual structure. The practiced eye can see at a glance the essential features of the horoscope, which in combination determine its structure. It is possible to speak of harmonious structure types when, for example, the general and individual structure correspond in their essential meanings. Such an example would be an emphasis in the spring signs occurring with a predominance of planets in the eastern half of the horoscope. Disharmonious structure types are found when the general and individual structure are unrelated, or contrary in nature. For example, an emphasis in the spring signs may occur in combination with a predominance of planets in the western half, or perhaps in the nocturnal half of the horoscope. The concepts of harmony and disharmony are not to be taken here as value judgments, however. Along with the appropriate dominant planets, both these structural types might further the development of creative ability, but in each case would do so in a different way. The problem is that where there is disharmony between the structural types the individual must learn to unite diverse tendencies in opposition within the personality.

An analysis of the vocational possibilities proceeds from an understanding of the interplay between structure and dominance. Structure represents those deep-seated, ineluctable tendencies that are made manifest by the power of the dominant planet, and in turn, the dominant planet receives from the structure its direction. For example, a dominant Mercury in combination with a preponderance of planets in the angular houses and the eastern half of the horoscope would be more strongly oriented to practical and material affairs than it would if combined with a preponderance of planets in the western half and in cadent houses, where the mental or intellectual facet of Mercury would come to the fore. The same planet dominant, in two different horoscopes, could result in two quite different vocations because structure gives to the dominant planet a different direction. The same applies to structure: similar structure in combination with different dominant planets can indicate different vocational areas.

For some vocations structure appears to be more decisive, while for others the dominant planets seem to be more so. Both elements are of importance in every case, but their relative strength depends on the particular vocation.

In the examples given in the book, the structural patterns as well as the dominant planets that are significant for a particular vocational area are described to the extent that present knowledge and research makes this possible. Astrological literature abounds in its interpretations of the particular elements of individual structure, but in most cases these are useless because they are in no way related to the dominant planets of the individual's horoscope.

Knowledge of Vocational Requirements

Along with an understanding of the general nature of a given personality, which is determined from the horoscope, a comprehension of the precise demands and requirements of the various vocational areas and professions is necessary if any worthwhile advice is to be given. A superficial grasp of what these requirements are will result in mistakes when one is faced with difficult cases, and at such times it is the astrologer and not astrology that is at fault.

Environmental and Other Outside Influences

A very difficult situation arises in those cases where parents or educators (or even the pressure of outward circumstances) determine the choice of profession without regard for the individual's interests and predilections. This danger is frequently seen among passive individuals who have no great abilities or strength of character; their horoscopes usually show strong unfavorable aspects. Frequently, this situation is mirrored in the horoscope by an adverse Saturn in the fourth or tenth house. In such cases it is possible to recommend a particular vocation only when there *are* indications of talent and favorable character traits that by their very strength enable the individual to overcome all barriers and obstacles. Hopefully, the astrologer can then assist in dissipating feelings of insecurity which may crystallize under the pressure of formidable persons or circumstances, and can hasten a development that would otherwise have only come about with greater delay.

At this point a few more words are in order concerning the influence of the environment. To a great extent it is believed that accurate evaluations of character, ability, vocation, etc. cannot be made if the individual's environment has not been taken into account. This is only partially correct. In reality, *very marked ability* in all cases is inexorably drawn to that milieu that corresponds to its own nature; but success is likely only when specific ability is combined with other favorable personality traits. When one encounters the horoscopes of such men and women, one sees clearly that for them talent is everything and environment is nothing. In the other categories it is true that if the environmental situation is not known, an evaluation is made much more difficult. Where general ability is lacking (group four), or is not very clearly defined (group two), or is a problem of no particular interest to the individual (group three), interpretation is difficult without knowledge of the environment. In all cases where the astrologer runs into these difficulties he must obtain knowledge of the general environmental circumstances. Anyway, those people whose cases are easy to evaluate almost never seek advice because really marked talent goes its own way without feeling the need for counsel; therefore, information concerning the environment should be requested at the start. The horoscopes showing outstanding ability must always be carefully studied, however, because such cases provide the clearest examples of basic principles of interpretation with which more difficult cases will be tested and compared. For this reason, the examples in the book include many horoscopes showing outstanding capability, and only at the end are a few cases of failure given for consideration.

Vocations

I have attempted to make clear—insofar as a knowledge of astrological tradition, my own compilation of statistics, and personal experience make possible—what kind of stellar configurations correspond to those traits of personality that seem significant for a given vocation. Great importance is placed on the *total* personality. In vocations where there is personal contact with many people, such as is usual among teachers, doctors, lawyers, etc., factors affecting social adjustment are important; in other cases, innate capabilities are alone decisive. Unfortunately, there has been very little written in the past about the relationship between interest and ability for a particular vocation and the underlying motivations in the personality, so it is not possible to consider the information here as necessarily complete.

The Learned Professions

The pursuit of knowledge for its own sake—so frequently an outstanding trait among the people of this group—is primarily a function of Mercury. One therefore finds Mercury strongly placed in the horoscope, in combination with other typical configurations that together indicate the particular area within this group. Those in the natural sciences will have a Mercury that has a somewhat different accent than those in liberal arts, and between these two general groups there are other differences as well that are adequately reflected in the horoscope. The true scholar will have a different Mercury than one for whom education has been only a means to a practical end—such as is the case among doctors, engineers, or clerics—and not for the sake of knowledge itself.

The learned professions are not determined solely by the strength of Mercury because first of all, Mercury must, as we shall see, not be too evidently dominant, and secondly, because confusion might arise with the indications of business talent, which is also associated with a strong Mercury. One may say that the scholar's Mercury must be strong, but not so completely dominant as is frequently found in the horoscopes of outstanding business people. Mercury in the first and tenth houses is seldom found in the horoscopes of scholars and intellectuals, but instead is usually several degrees *before* the cusp of those houses. It is frequently found in the seventh or fourth house, and even more frequently in strong aspect to the Midheaven or Ascendant. If there is a more practical turn of mind, such as one might expect among engineers or inventors, Mercury then is often found in the first or tenth house.

The principle seems to be that a planet that is just *ahead* of the cusp of an angular house, but still actually in conjunction with it (within an orb of up to seven degrees), will express itself in a mental or intellectual way. This principle should not be confused with the one described by F. Glahn and other astrologers whereby a planet in the last ten degrees of *any* house is considered to take on this mental accentuation. Rather, as already stated, the conjunction of a planet with an angular cusp will indicate a more mental mode of action when the planet is *before* the angular house cusp than would be so if the planet were actually *in* the angular house. This is more evident in the case of the tenth or first house because these houses incline by their nature to pragmatic, positive, and more extroverted expression. By contrast, planets in the fourth and seventh houses are more introverted in their action and frequently find their best release in mental activity. The true scholar does not have many planets in the first and tenth houses because these have too strong a tendency to outward activity and the conduct of affairs than would be appropriate in the pursuit of knowledge. Even the natural scientist is no exception here, despite the fact that in most cases his horoscope will show a predominance of planets in the eastern half of the horoscope. For men of learning with a more practical orientation such as doctors, this principle is not applicable.

In these learned professions one frequently finds that both favorable and unfavorable aspects between planets indicating talent have about the same effect. With favorable aspects, the capabilities shown by the planets mesh with each other in a natural and harmonious way, whereas with unfavorable aspects, the capabilities shown operate in disharmony. Only after considerable struggle within the individual personality can any accomplishments be expected. Because they are born of conflict, these efforts often show great depth of insight and profound significance, while at the same time a forced intensity and a dogmatic insistence. Very often in those cases of disharmonious aspects between planets that show a specific talent, conflict with the Zeitgeist or with official opinion is the result, and an unfortunate shadow is cast over the individual's career and destiny. But persons with such configurations are capable, through concentration and labor, of making fruitful the contradictions of their nature and of bringing all their talents to bear on the problem. It is they who in the end are able to destroy established opinion so that new paths of knowledge may be found.

The Natural Sciences

Professions that deal with the more *theoretical* side—with investigation and experimentation—should incorporate a sense of objectivity, a gift for careful analysis, a critical attitude, logic, a talent for experimentation, and perhaps intuition. One generally finds an emphasis on the earth or even the water signs, a strong but not too outgoing Mercury, and planets in the third house (interest in science). For the more practical application of these professions, general character traits will be equally decisive and these must be considered separately in each case; generally, there are more planets in the signs occupying the angles.

The Chemist

Tradition speaks of a strong Scorpio influence and a strong Mars. Frankly, I am not sure what the deep-seated motives are that result in an interest in chemistry or chemical research. One would expect a predominance of the scientific signs as well as a strong Mercury; for theoretical application, an emphasis on the air signs; and on the earth signs for more practical and experimental application.

With respect to practical application, the particular area of interest is important and sometimes can be recognized by studying the angular houses. In any case, there are very few horoscopes of chemists available and the following examples should be considered as having only limited value.

Example 1: Doctor of Chemistry, October 2, 1866, 2:00 a.m., 54N30, 13E13

10th 13 ♉	☉ 8 ♎ 30	♃ 22 ♑ 42
11th 23 ♊	☽ 18 ♋ 50	♂ 12 ♋
12th 29 ♋	♆ 11 ♈ 30	♀ 25 ♏
1st 26 ♌	♅ 8 ♋ 30	☿ 7 ♎ 40
2nd 15 ♍	♄ 10 ♏ 50	
3rd 10 ♎		

Saturn, the strongest planet in the horoscope and in Scorpio, receives a trine from Mars in the water sign Cancer in the eleventh house. Mars is conjunct the Moon and Uranus and sextile the tenth house cusp. The Sun and Mercury are in the third house, showing the interest in science.

Example 2: Doctor of Chemistry, October 19, 1898, 7:30 p.m., 50N50, 12E53

10th 16 ♒	☉ 26 ♎ 24	♃ 21 ♎ 54
11th 15 ♓	☽ 22 ♐ 01	♂ 25 ♋ 17
12th 0 ♉	♆ 24 ♊ 41	♀ 8 ♐ 59

1st 21 ♊ ♅ 1 ♐ 37 ☿ 22 ♎ 24

2nd 9 ♋ ♄ 9 ♐ 25 ☊ 12 ♑ 22

3rd 26 ♋

The Ascendant, Neptune, Jupiter, Sun, and Mercury are all in the scientific signs, Gemini and Libra, and form strong and favorable aspects to each other. Mars in Cancer in the third house receives many strong aspects; the one from Uranus is probably the most significant.

Pharmacology is an important area of applied chemistry, but the horoscopes of druggists reveal business interests, which are usually found in the second house; frequently the Sun or the Moon is there. The horoscope of the apothecary who aspires to be something more than a shopkeeper will show a strong Scorpio element; there is some similarity here with the horoscopes of physicians.

Example 1: Pharmacist, born December 16, 1876, 4:15 a.m., 51N31, 1E9

The water sign Scorpio is on the Ascendant (see page 16) and Mars rises in the same sign, clearly showing an interest in medicine and a genuine desire to cure the sick. As we shall see later, the sign Scorpio is quite characteristic of an interest in medicine and chemotherapy, often found in combination with a talent for teaching. Business interests are shown by Jupiter, Sun, Mercury, and the Moon occupying the second house, and the trines formed to these planets by Uranus in the tenth house indicate a willingness to utilize the latest discoveries in his field without hesitation, as well as indicating a good intuitive faculty.*

Example 2: Doctor of Pharmaceutics, born July 11, 1864, 2:55 a.m., 50N30, 12E15

---

*Von Klockler has already discussed the great importance he ascribes to a planet placed just before the cusp of an angular house. The reader will note that in this and several other instances, von Klockler considers that such a planet is then *in* the angular house.

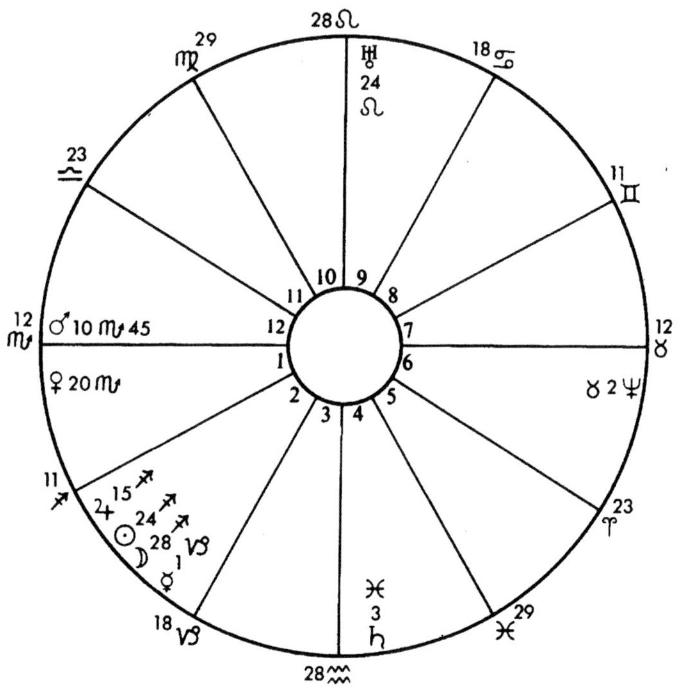

Example 1, Pharmacist

10th 1 ♓	☉ 18 ♋ 56	♂ 1 ♉
11th 4 ♈	☽ 6 ♎ 43	♀ 17 ♋
12th 21 ♉	♆ 8 ♈	☿ 11 ♋
1st 4 ♋	♅ 27 ♊	☊ 15 ♏
2nd 20 ♋	♄ 12 ♎	
3rd 8 ♌	♃ 18 ♏	

The Ascendant, Sun, and Mercury are in the water sign Cancer, and the Sun and Venus are in the second house trine to Jupiter in Scorpio in the sixth. Mars in the eleventh house is sextile the Ascendant, Midheaven and Uranus.

The Physicist

This vocation demands an extraordinary love of science. The knowledge of physics necessary for the study of other sciences may not require much ability beyond the average, but the true physicist could not be satisfied with that; he is, above all, a man of research. Varying forms of expression are found in this area too.

There may be an emphasis on intuition or on abstract mathematics, and the horoscope will show to which of these two groups the individual belongs *primarily,* since clearly he must have some ability for both. The capacity for intuitive insight comes usually from a strong Jupiter, and particularly from Mercury-Jupiter aspects; the capacity for experimentation and its more technical application will be shown through a predominance of the earth signs and a strong Uranus. The Sun, Mercury, or Ascendant may be in earth signs, or the planet of greatest influence may be in one.

The interest in scientific research is seen in an emphasis on the scientific signs and in planets occupying the third house. Mercury must of course be strong, and is usually found to be so through *aspects* to the angular cusps rather than by location in the angular houses. Moreover, Mercury is frequently in aspect to Venus and Uranus, and my experience shows it is usually found in the cardinal signs, but not necessarily so.

Example 1: Prof. Otto Wiener, Director of the Physics Institute at the University of Leipzig, June 15, 1892, 2:00 a.m., 49N, 8E30

The interest in science, whose ideal is after all to understand and to regulate into a comprehensive order the vast world of perceptible reality, is seen by the Ascendant (see page 18) in the earth sign Taurus. The third house (specific scientific interests) is emphasized by the position of Mercury.

Mercury in the third house is very strong because it still remains within orb of its conjunction with the IC. It can be considered co-ruler of the horoscope, and it also has a sextile to the ascending

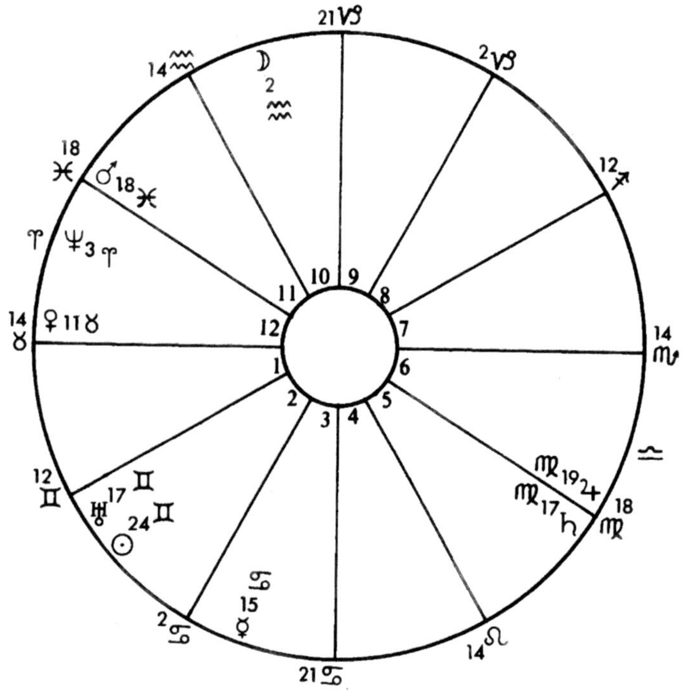

Example 1, Physicist

degree and to Venus rising there. Mercury receives other strong aspects: the sextile from Saturn increases the sense of objectivity, depth of thought, and logic, while the sextile from Jupiter shows intuition and imagination. The trine of Mercury to Mars shows powers of self-expression that are both lively and persuasive, a talent for teaching, and a skill and dexterity that are indispensable in experimental physics. The versatility of this man, who, among other things, has occupied himself with both theoretical and practical problems in aeronautics, is shown by the Gemini Sun (communication, connection, relationship) and particularly by its conjunction with Uranus in that sign.

Venus a few degrees ahead of the ascending degree is an indication of the very kindly disposition of this man, but is not in itself strong enough to outweigh the powerful Mercury.

Example 2: Prof. des Coudres, Director of the Institute for Theoretical Physics at the University of Leipzig, March 13, 1862, 3:00 a.m., 52N, 9E15

10th 8 ♏	☉ 22 ♓	♃ 23 ♍
11th 29 ♏	☽ 12 ♌	♂ 15 ♑
12th 15 ♐	♆ 1 ♈	♀ 0 ♓
1st 2 ♑	♅ 13 ♊	☿ 29 ♒ 40
2nd 20 ♒	♄ 19 ♍	
3rd 7 ♈		

In this horoscope we also find an emphasis on the third house through the presence of the Sun and Neptune (consider the horoscope without the inner house divisions and compare it with the previous example). Capricorn on the Ascendant inclines to an interest in the natural sciences. As is often the case in the horoscopes of outstanding mathematicians, physicists, and astronomers, Mercury is conjunct Venus, and what is more important in this instance, is exactly sextile the Ascendant.

Example 3: Johannes Kepler, January 6, 1571, 2:30 p.m.

This great astronomer (see page 20) has the scientific sign Gemini on the Ascendant and, as a sort of counterweight, a group of planets in the earth sign Capricorn, which as we have said inclines to an interest in the natural sciences. Mercury is conjunct Uranus, a common feature in the horoscopes of physicists, mathematicians, and astronomers, and is in Capricorn in the seventh house; this configuration rules the horoscope. My statistics show Mercury in Capricorn to be frequent in the horoscopes of this group. Furthermore, Mercury is sextile Saturn, giving good objectivity, logic, and depth of thought. The square of Mercury to Mars gives a talent

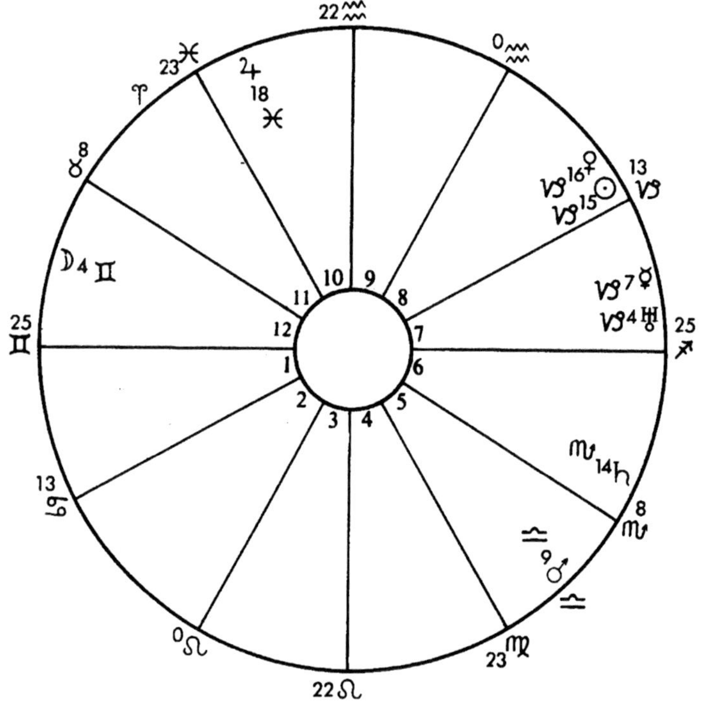

Example 3, Johannes Kepler

for dialectics which is most evident from Kepler's many polemical writings. The preponderance of planets in the western half of the horoscope—in particular the seventh and eighth houses—is reminiscent of the horoscopes of philosophers, and actually there was much of the philosopher in Kepler, a fact that was ignored by generations of scientists that followed him, but is now receiving more attention. In this horoscope, however, I find no indication of the *specific* area of scientific talent.

Example 4: Isaac Newton, January 4, 1643 (according to 1001 Notable Nativities by Alan Leo)

10th 27 ♋	☉ 14 ♑	♃ 14 ♓
11th 2 ♍	☽ 2 ♋	♂ 7 ♉
12th 29 ♍	♆ 1 ♐ 30	♀ 27 ♒
1st 20 ♎	♅ 15 ♏ 30	☿ 21 ♐
2nd 16 ♏	♄ 20 ♓	
3rd 19 ♐		

The scientific sign Libra rises and the third house (pursuit of knowledge, analysis) contains both Mercury and the Sun. Mercury is the most significant planet and has an exact sextile to the Ascendant and is, as in the first two examples, in aspect to Venus, in this case by sextile. Mercury's aspects to Saturn and Jupiter indicate logic, objectivity, and depth of thought, as well as intuition. As with Kepler, the Sun is in the earth sign Capricorn, showing interest in the *natural* sciences. Originality is indicated by the Sun in aspect to Uranus. The interest in mysticism, which Newton showed in the latter part of his life, is seen in the trine of Neptune to the Midheaven.

The Physician

The first observation to be made is that the horoscopes of physicians can show angular house placements.

Most will agree that the desire to heal the sick ought to be present in all physicians. But it must be pointed out that the desire can result from a desire for power, which is very easily gratified in the practice of a medical career. This explains the tradition that a physician's horoscope should have a strong Mars. Mars is the symbol of the struggle to power by infringement, interference, correction, and activity in general as opposed to knowledge and creative ability, which are functions of Jupiter. That this ancient rule still is a good one is perhaps not self-explanatory, however. In the era when astrology was first developed, physicians and surgeons were one and the same, and the physician was moreover predominantly a surgeon and was summoned even for such relatively minor treatment as bloodletting. Therefore, one might assume that only surgeons would have this marked influence of Mars in their horoscopes, but that is by no means the case and in almost all horoscopes of physicians, Mars is prominent, either by being in an angular house or exactly aspecting an angular house cusp. The difference between so-called favorable and unfavorable aspects is here—as in most instances of determining sheer ability—negligible, and unfavorable aspects confer the same ability as favorable. In the case of unfavorable aspects, however, the temperament is more disagreeable and cutting and reveals a greater disharmony arising from ambition and the striving for power, which can lead to differences of opinion with professional colleagues and other similar difficulties. Perhaps in these cases, as is frequently true, unfavorable aspects really indicate an overcompensation for a fundamental lack of ability or appropriate character traits. Moreover, Mars is as a rule in the sixth or twelfth house, and usually conjunct some planet—often Mercury or Venus.

The concept of a strong Mars should not be taken in a too narrow sense. For example, Mars may be in the eleventh house without aspect to either the Ascendant or Midheaven and yet be in exact aspect to a first house planet which is the strongest planet in the horoscope. (This is particularly true when the planet in the first house cannot be immediately linked to any vocation, such as the Sun, Moon, Mercury, and perhaps also Saturn. Venus, by contrast, almost always has reference to the vocation when located in the first house.)

This Mars element can, in those cases where it appears to be deficient, be replaced by a prominence of the Martian signs Aries or Scorpio. The typical sign of the physician is Scorpio, and Aries for the surgeon. In this respect, the physician's horoscope bears similarities with that of the teacher; both have authority, which is one of the considerable satisfactions of each profession. There is perhaps some similarity with the horoscopes of ministers and clerics, as these also have a strong Scorpio element—particularly Mercury in Scorpio. In this latter vocation, authority doubtless plays an important role, and the minister is a healer as well, though in a different sense.

The strong Mars, or Scorpio element, is not all that goes into making the physician, however, and it has been noted that the horoscopes of physicians and their patients often have much in common, such as planets located in the sixth and twelfth houses. There may be a clue here to the real reason the medical profession is chosen as it seems possible that some physical or nervous disorder leads to an awareness of the gravity of illness, and this in turn produces the desire to cure others. The doctor-to-be experiences some inner conflict resulting from a recognition of his own illness and this personal experience then becomes generalized into the desire to help others. In any case, the fact that so many physicians have planets in the sixth and twelfth houses cannot be without significance, and our interpretation seems justified, though it may not yet be proved. The simplistic formula—"asylums, hospitals, prisons"=—for the twelfth house is of course well-known and in fact the Sun and Moon, as well as other horoscope factors, are frequently found in the sixth or twelfth houses in many physicians' and psychiatrists' horoscopes. (As we shall see later, there is some possibility here of confusion with the twelfth house placements associated with the criminal lawyer.)

Among bacteriologists, pathologists, physiologists, and those occupied with hygienics or medical research, the astrological situation is not much different, except that more abstract scientific interests are found subjoined to the medical. In addition to what has been said, Mercury will be prominent (but not usually in the first or tenth house), as will the third house (Pasteur had six planets in the third house and Mercury in aspect to the Ascendant).

It is not now possible to determine the field of specialization in medicine from the horoscope, and it is a moot question whether at any time in the future it will be possible to extract further details of this sort from the horoscope since in many cases it is opportunity that dictates the choice of the field of specialization, even when the conflict involving illness outlined above has nothing to do with the field chosen. It is quite possible that, for example, a predisposition to eye disease would produce the ophthalmologist, but for details of this sort a thorough astrological study of disease and illness would be necessary, and there is none available at present. Nevertheless, a general interest in either internal medicine, psychiatry, or surgery can be read from the horoscope.

My statistics show that psychiatrists frequently have Moon-Neptune contacts. Neurologists, who frequently specialize in mental rather than strictly anatomical ailments, show important placements in the fifth house. The fifth house has affinity with certain basic personality *drives,* an evaluation of which is so important in disturbances of this kind. These fifth house positions may indicate pedagogical talent as well.

Surgeons have a stronger Mars, usually posited in an angular house and preferably the tenth or first, but the sixth house is also found. Mars has many aspects, particularly to the Sun or Moon, and often to Mercury. There is frequently a strong Aries element. The signs Scorpio and Virgo, on the other hand, are most frequently found in the horoscope of the internal medicine specialist.

Example 1: Internal medicine specialist, November 4, 1887, 7:30 a.m., 50N, 0E27

The Ascendant (see page 25) is in Scorpio—a common feature in the horoscopes of doctors—and the Sun and Jupiter are close to the rising degree; but most significant of all is Mars in the tenth house sextile the Scorpio planets. The strong Scorpio element explains the interest in medicine and healing the sick, and confers a gift for teaching.

Example 2: Specialist in nervous disorders, September 1, 1882, 2:00 p.m., 51N30, 0E27

10th 11 ♎ ☉ 8 ♍ 57 ♃ 27 ♊ 51
11th 5 ♏ ☽ 0 ♉ 40 ♂ 9 ♎

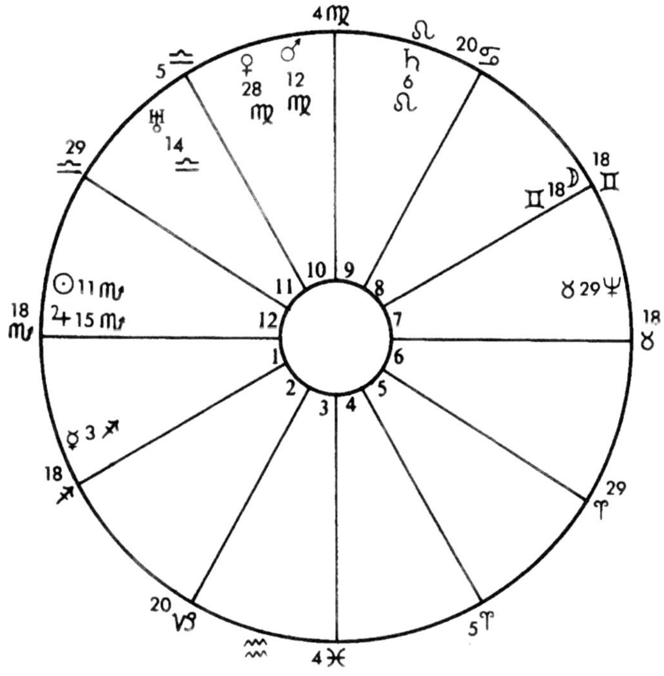

Example 1, Internal Medicine Specialist

12th 25 ♏ ♆ 18 ♉ 49 ♀ 23 ♎ 45
1st 11 ♐ ♅ 18 ♍ 19 ☿ 27 ♍ 17
2nd 18 ♑ ♄ 26 ♉ 08
3rd 4 ♓

Mars just before the cusp of the tenth house rules the horoscope and is sextile the Ascendant; in the air sign Libra it shows an intellectual bent. The planets in the ninth house in the scientific sign Virgo, and the Moon and Neptune in the fifth house, show at the same time the interest in man's instinctual life and the possibility of transcending it through a more spiritual point of view. Successful psychiatrists and neurologists often have a strong Jupiter, indicating that personal difficulties are relived to some extent through the professional life. It also indicates great trust and faith on the part of one's patients.

Example 3: Neurologist, April 4, 1876, 9:30 p.m., 49N, 0E34

10th 4 ♍	☉ 16 ♈ 25	♃ 1 ♐ 37
11th 5 ♎	☽ 26 ♌ 52	♂ 25 ♉ 25
12th 29 ♎	♆ 2 ♉ 06	♀ 28 ♉ 30
1st 18 ♏	♅ 16 ♌ 03	☿ 28 ♓ 16
2nd 18 ♐	♄ 3 ♓ 55	
3rd 25 ♑		

Scorpio is again rising and Mars is strong in the seventh house, showing energy directed to mental or intellectual pursuits, and is also in aspect to the very powerful first house Jupiter. The fifth house contains the Sun and Mercury, while the ninth has the Moon and Uranus. Compassion as well as the desire to cure the sick is shown by the first house Jupiter in aspect to Mercury on the fifth house cusp and to the Moon in the ninth house.

Example 4: Physician, October 13, 1901, 10:45 p.m., 5lN, 0E50

10th 1 ♈	☉ 19 ♎ 51	♃ 6 ♑ 09
11th 10 ♉	☽ 4 ♏ 40	♂ 29 ♏ 33
12th 23 ♊	♆ 1 ♋ 28	♀ 1 ♐ 18
1st 27 ♋	♅ 14 ♐ 01	☿ 14 ♏ 41
2nd 13 ♌	♄ 10 ♑ 29	
3rd 3 ♍		

Scorpio is again emphasized through the position of the Moon and Mercury, but most significant is Mars in Scorpio in the fifth house in exact trine to both the Ascendant and the Midheaven. Without this strong Mars one might easily conclude from this horoscope that teaching would be the most suitable profession and in fact the primary interest of this physician is child hygiene and the treatment of disturbed children. The interest in psychiatry is shown by the Moon trine Neptune. Saturn, Jupiter, and Neptune are in the sixth or twelfth houses, showing the identification and subjective rapport with disease.

Example 5: Professor of Psychiatry, August 28, 1875, 7:00 a.m., 45N, 0E47

In this horoscope (see page 28) we see several planets in the twelfth house in the scientific sign Virgo, while Mars rules the horoscope from the fourth house, inclining this planet to a more subjective form of expression. Its square to the Ascendant and aspects to Jupiter, Sun, Venus, Neptune, and Saturn all show the basic interest in medicine. The unfavorable Moon-Neptune aspect mentioned earlier as a typical feature of the horoscopes of psychiatrists occurs here as a square, and Neptune is at the same time in the eighth house, and in aspect with the Sun, Venus, and Mercury in the twelfth house.

Following are some random notes of interest concerning several horoscopes of physicians:

Example 6: Dr. Carl Ludwig Schleich, surgeon. Mars conjunct the Sun on the cusp of the tenth house rules the horoscope.

Example 7: General practitioner. Mercury in Capricorn in the first house is the dominant planet. It receives a trine from Mars in Virgo.

Example 8: General practitioner. The Ascendant receives an exact trine from Mars.

Example 9: Dermatologist. The Sun is in Scorpio in the twelfth house, and the Moon is in Taurus in the sixth. Mars in Sagittarius in the first house is the strongest planet.

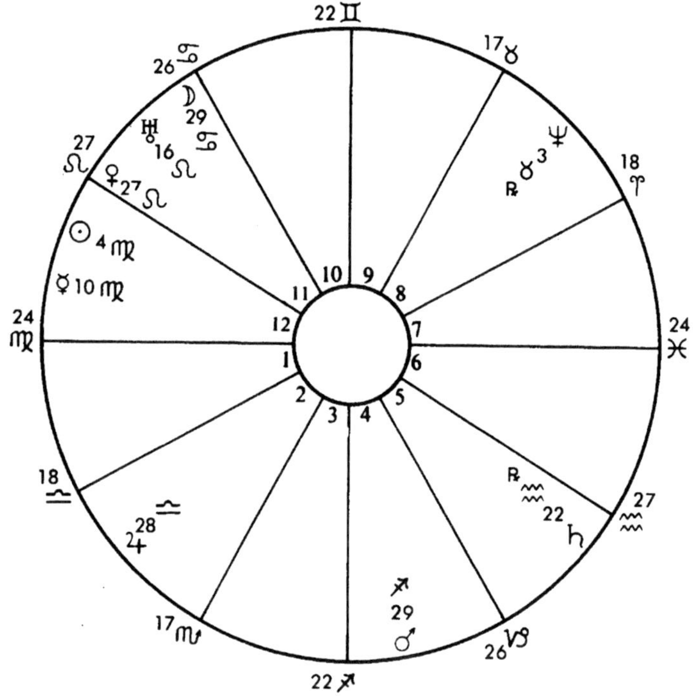

Example 5, Professor of Psychiatry

Example 10: General practitioner and obstetrician. The Ascendant, Saturn and Uranus are in Scorpio. Mars in the first house is the strongest planet.

Example 11: General practitioner. Mars is in Scorpio in the fifth house and trine both the Ascendant and Midheaven. The Sun is in Scorpio. The Moon is in the twelfth house, while Venus and Mercury are in the sixth.

Example 12: General practitioner. The Sun is in Scorpio in the eleventh house. Mercury and the Moon are in the twelfth house, with the latter in aspect to Mars. There is no aspect here between Mars and an angular cusp.

Example 13: Surgeon. The surgical sign Aries rises with Jupiter in the Ascendant. Mercury, Uranus, Sun, Venus and Mars are in the sixth house.

Example 14: Professor and director of the dental institute at a German University. The Ascendant is in the surgical sign Aries. Mars in Capricorn in the tenth house rules the horoscope and is in aspect to Mercury (manual dexterity), Venus, Neptune, and Uranus (interest in technology).

The Engineer

The particular talent for technology that we are concerned with here is what I will call inventive ability. Characteristic of this ability is a strong aspect between Mercury and Uranus. A strong Uranus in the horoscope is not by itself sufficient, although it is in fact usually found to be strong. Superior ability for technology definitely requires a powerful Mercury and this is provided by either its position in an angular house, aspect to an angular cusp, or aspect to another planet in an angular house, which for the proper strength, should in turn be located in at least the first two-thirds of that house.

In the area of more practical application, Mercury is best placed in either the first or tenth house. Technological ability is clearly based on a capacity for intellectual analysis and a flare for mechanics, which underlie all work in this field, and these are best understood as Mercury functions. Manual dexterity and a general adroitness are required for the carrying out of experiments. This knack or feeling for technology can be expressed in several ways: an emphasis on Libra or Aquarius, Mercury-Mars aspects, and Mars-Uranus aspects (see also the section on The Mechanic).

Inventive ability demands more, however, than just a knack for mechanics and some ability for analytical thinking. It also requires intuition and rapid comprehension. In short, Uranus must be strongly placed, and this is best seen—but not exclusively seen—by a Mercury-Uranus aspect, although it is also allowable that these planets be found prominent by some separate relationship to the angular houses without actually being in mutual aspect.

Although in general the so-called critical aspects confer as much ability as the favorable ones, an exception must be made in the case of the inventor. With either kind of aspect the degree of ability may be the same, but the unfavorable aspects are a sign that the inventive vision may be too distant and impractical, so that opposition and resistance in the environment is excessive and such problems as lack of financial backing will arise. The inventor is condemned to unfruitfulness; his ideas are not timely.

The particular area of specialization in engineering cannot be seen from the horoscope and there are no formulas and no generally valid principles from which to deduce details. In any particular case a general consideration of the character, and in particular the kind of general mentality shown (Sun sign and house), as well as the particular direction of the intellect and intuition (Mercury and Uranus by sign and house), may provide the correct clues. For the present, however, we must be content to be able solely to discern a gift for invention and a general interest in technology in the horoscope. The broad indications are known, and only future research will provide the information needed for the reading of details.

Mathematical ability, which is usually a requisite for engineers, is seen in Mercury-Uranus aspects as well as Mercury-Saturn aspects.

Example 1: Marconi, born April 25, 1874, 4:50 p.m., 44N, 45E

In this horoscope we find Libra rising, indicating the possibility of an interest in technology. But the most outstanding indication of Marconi's inventive genius is the Mercury-Uranus trine, which rules the horoscope. Mercury is in the cardinal sign Aries—a position that seems to further mathematical and technological ability—is conjunct the cusp of the seventh house, and is to be taken as

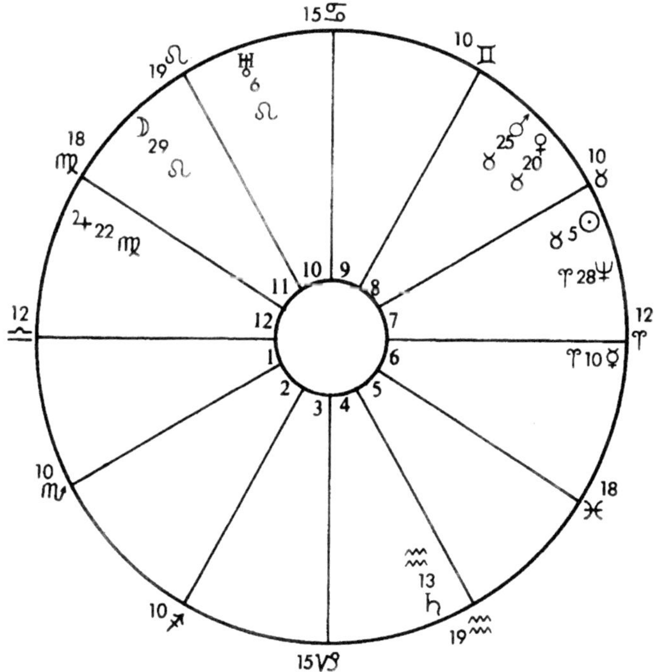

Example 1, Marconi

the dominant single factor in the horoscope. Uranus is in the middle of the tenth house (profession), but even more important is its sextile to the Ascendant. Moreover, Mercury is sextile Saturn, giving mathematical ability.

Note: This horoscope was first given by Dr. Uhle in *Die Fixsterne* and only recently I learned that it is a speculative one done by an astrologer in Vienna. The time of birth does not correspond with the official time given to me subsequently by Dr. W. Mrsic of April 25, 1874, 9:00 a.m. in Griffone near Bologna. The data for this time are:

10th 17 ♓	☉ 4 ♉ 55	♄ 13 ♒ 38
11th 22 ♈	☽ 25 ♌ 20	♃ 22 ♍ 39
12th 5 ♊	♆ 28 ♈ 32	♂ 24 ♉ 57
1st 12 ♋	♅ 6 ♌ 33	♀ 20 ♉ 14
2nd 0 ♌		☿ 9 ♈ 27
3rd 20 ♌		

The author of the speculative horoscope rightly concluded that the typical inventor aspect should be dominant, but of the four or five possible times this could happen during the day of birth, he selected the incorrect one. In both horoscopes Mercury is dominant—here in the tenth house square the Ascendant. In the speculative horoscope, it is in the seventh house in opposition to the Ascendant. However, the other aspects have unequal strength in the two horoscopes. Compare also this horoscope with Example 2 given just after Marconi's in the text. In both cases Mercury is in the tenth house trine Uranus in the second. albeit in different signs.

Example 2: Engineer, August 1, 1905, 1:00 p.m., Dresden

10th 21 ♌	☉ 8 ♌ 32	♃ 2 ♊
11th 24 ♍	☽ 12 ♌ 51	♂ 20 ♏
12th 19 ♎	♆ 9 ♋	♀ 25 ♊
1st 8 ♏	♅ 1 ♋	☿ 6 ♍
2nd 7 ♐	♄ 1 ♓	
3rd 12 ♑		

In this horoscope Mercury in Virgo in the tenth house is dominant, and in a position favorable for analytical thought. Its sextile to Neptune, opposition to Saturn, and square to Jupiter are less an indication of this man's profession than the sextile from Uranus in the second house. The sextiles from the eighth house planets to Mercury in the tenth house are to be considered of primary importance. This man, though still quite young, has produced several useful and worthwhile inventions.

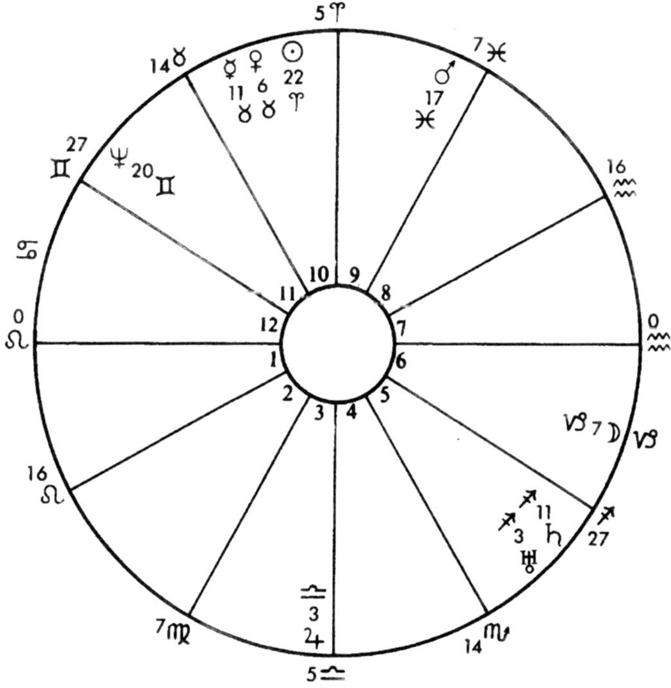

Example 3, Engineer

Example 3: Engineer, April 12, 1898, 51N, 0E55

Uranus is the most important planet through its trine to the Midheaven and Ascendant. Although not in any relationship with an angular house cusp, Mercury is strong by its aspects to Mars and the Moon, so we find that the conditions for mastering the technological and mathematical problems of the vocation are at hand. This is the horoscope of a well-known construction designer.

Example 4: Engineer, June 28, 1895, 8:30 p.m., 51N, 0E55

10th 15 ♏ ☉ 7 ♋ 30 ♃ 15 ♋

11th 5 ♐ ☽ 27 ♍ ♂ 11 ♌

12th 22 ♐	♆ 16 ♊ 30	♀ 22 ♌
1st 4 ♑	♅ 16 ♏	☿ 11 ♋
2nd 1 ♓	♄ 0 ♏ 30	
3rd 17 ♈		

Mercury in the cardinal sign Cancer is strongly placed in the seventh house and is trine Uranus in Scorpio in the tenth house. This is the horoscope of a successful engineer in the field of heating equipment.

Liberal Arts

The Philosopher

Every man has his own philosophy and there are as many philosophies as there are philosophers. Nevertheless, an interest in philosophy is described by quite specific factors, which must be present in some degree of strength in the philosopher's horoscope. A good intellect, logic, a capacity for abstract theory, and a reflective or contemplative nature are indispensable. In addition, objectivity and an ability for mathematical or natural sciences, as well as imagination and a religious outlook, may also be present but are not absolutely necessary.

In the horoscopes of the greatest philosophers—and we present their horoscopes here as a guide in the judgment of the not-so-great—we find the possibility of increased intellectual power in an emphasis on the scientific signs Gemini, Virgo, Libra, Scorpio, and Aquarius. The Ascendant, the dominant planet, or a group of planets are usually found in one of these signs, and this agrees with the statistics reported by the French astrologer Flambart for 800 *esprits superieurs*. Further, we frequently find Mercury-Moon contacts which, whether favorable or unfavorable, apparently contribute to intellectual development.

Logic and a sense of objectivity, which are particularly necessary for philosophers who develop theories of cognition, are recognized by Mercury-Saturn aspects, whereas the more intuitive philosopher will have Mercury-Uranus aspects. In all cases Mercury must be strongly placed, either in an angular house (the seventh and fourth are better than the first and tenth), or in aspect to an angular cusp. In cases where Mercury is close to the first or tenth house cusp, I find that it is almost always just in front of the cusp of those houses.

The reflective temperament characteristic of almost all philosophers is seen through the predominance of planets in the western half of the horoscope. Interest in metaphysics is a particular feature of the sign Scorpio, while the desire to establish an all-encompassing world view is shown by appropriate planets in the ninth house. There are exceptions to this, but they are rare. Nietzsche, for example, who was actually more of a prophet than a philosopher, had a majority of planets in the eastern side of the horoscope, but in the autumn signs, showing that a basically reflective temperament was projected into outward activity. The reverse situation—the planets in the western half of the horoscope in the spring and summer signs—leads to tension and conflict, the tendency to feel oneself an outsider (Kayserling, Spengler), and perhaps an interest in the natural sciences.

Example 1: K.E. Johannes Vaihinger, September 25, 1852, 4:30 p.m., Zahren near Tubingen

The horoscope shows the scientific sign Aquarius on the Ascendant, while Mercury, Sun, Mars, and Jupiter are in Virgo, Libra, and Scorpio and therefore all in scientific signs. Without looking further, it can be said that these placements help further intellectuality. The majority of planets are in the western half of the horoscope and in the autumn signs, showing the basically reflective temperament. Mercury is in the congenial sign Virgo in the seventh house and is at least the second strongest planet in the horoscope. The intellectual and analytical tendency of Virgo (Virgo: perpendicular, intensive thinking as opposed to horizontal, extensive thinking) is emphasized here and Mercury aspects Saturn (ob-

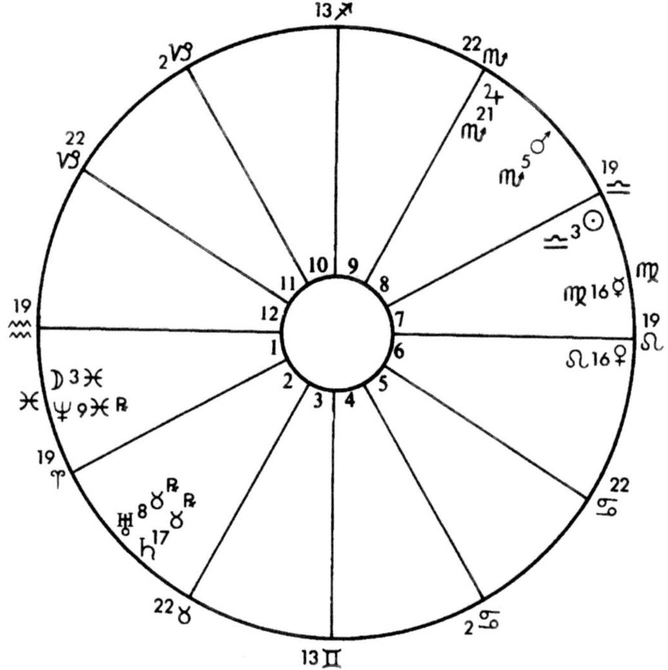

Example 1, K.E. Johannes Vaihinger

jectivity, logic) and is sextile Jupiter in the ninth, another position that reveals a predilection for philosophy.

The "as-if" philosophy of Vaihinger is concerned primarily with the role and meaning of illusion in human thought, and the planets in the western half of the horoscope of this philosopher, who is also a natural scientist. However, the planets in the spring and summer signs point up the elements of practicality, utility, and organization, which are easily recognizable in Wundt's work. Mercury conjunct the Moon and Neptune in his horoscope is an apt symbol of such a point of view. As we know, Neptune is the planet of Maya—of illusion.

Example 2: Hans Driesch, October 28, 1867, 5:00 p.m., Kreuznach

10th 20 ♑	☉ 5 ♏	♃ 28 ♒
11th 12 ♒	☽ 18 ♏	♂ 22 ♏ 30
12th 16 ♓	♆ 13 ♈	♀ 13 ♏ 30
1st 14 ♉	♅ 13 ♋	☿ 28 ♏
2nd 13 ♊	♄ 24 ♏	
3rd 2 ♋		

The horoscope contains many planets in Scorpio, one of the scientific signs, and a possible indication of a superior intellect, as well as an interest in metaphysics. The predominance of planets in the western half of the horoscope, and especially the seventh house, is very striking, and the more so as an autumn sign is involved. Mercury is strong in the seventh house, and its conjunction with Saturn shows logic and objectivity. This and the fact that Taurus rises explains the empirical orientation of this philosopher as well as his interest in the natural sciences. The conjunction of Mercury and Mars sharpens the wits and makes one disputatious, and at the same time confers a talent for teaching and oratory. particularly since Mercury is in Scorpio. The conjunction of Mercury and the Moon is outside the allowable orb but can be considered effective as they are both conjunct Mars and Saturn, which act as intermediaries; this is a further indication of intellectuality. The square of Mercury to Jupiter can be considered in this case to support the power of Mercury, while originality and intuition are shown by the strong aspects Uranus throws to the Ascendant, Sun, Moon, and Venus.

Example 3: Wilhelm Wundt, August 16, 1832, 2:00 p.m., Neckarau near Mannheim

Once again a reflective temperament is suggested by the many planets in the western half of the horoscope of this philosopher who is also a natural scientist. However, the planets in the spring

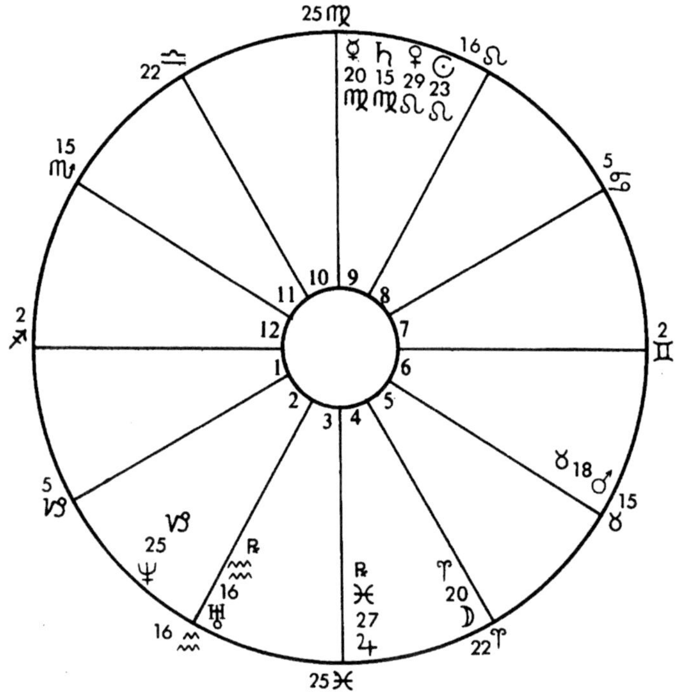

Example 3, Wilhelm Wundt

and summer signs point up the elements of practicality, utility, and organization, which are recognizable in Wundt's work. Mercury, planet of intellectuality and rationality, is close to the tenth house cusp in Virgo (analysis) but is actually in the ninth house; its conjunction with Saturn indicates, as in the above cases cited, logic and objectivity. The ninth house planets also show the interest in philosophy and the impulse to unify diverse areas of knowledge. The trine of Mercury to Mars confers a talent for teaching as well as for debate. The trine of Mercury to Neptune shows in interest in psychology, as does the aspect between the Moon and Neptune. However, the square of the Sun in the ninth house to Mars reveals a dogmatic attitude.

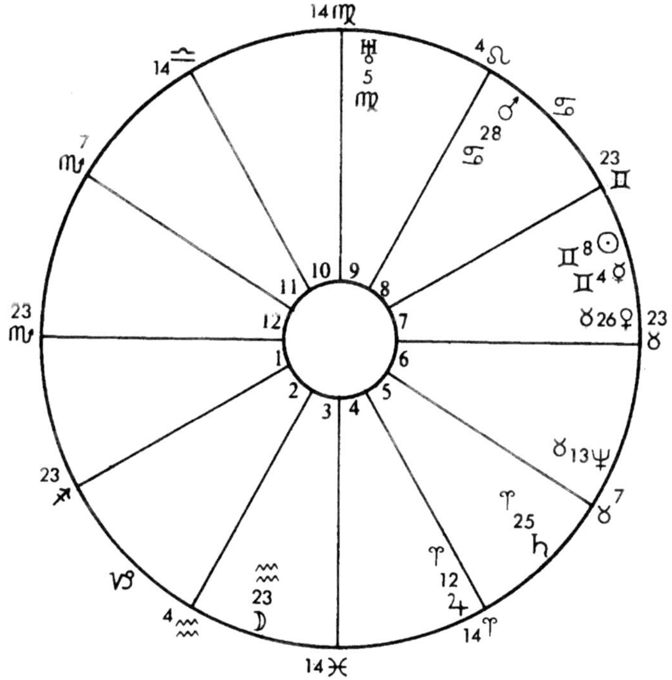

Example 4, Oswald Spengler

Example 4: Oswald Spengler, May 29, 1880, 6:30 p.m., Blankenburg

The Ascendant, Sun, Moon, Uranus, and Mercury are in scientific signs. Mercury in Gemini in the seventh house shows the high degree of intellectuality. Again we see that almost all planets are in the reflective western half of the horoscope. Mercury is placed very close to the Sun (four degrees distant) and has no relationship to Saturn, indicating subjectivity of thought. The planets in Gemini represent the urge to establish intellectual connections, relationships, and bridges, and indicate the wide scope and diversification of his thought. The square of Mercury to Uranus in the ninth house indicates intuition in philosophical matters, but put to use with difficulty or under strain. The sextile of Mercury to Mars confers a talent for dialectics, while the sextile of Mercury to Jupiter gives what one might best call an intellectual instinct. All these things are true, of course, only because Mercury is so strong.

The Teacher

A distinction must always be made between the teacher of a specialized subject at a higher institution and the teacher who is concerned with the overall formative education of a much younger age group. In the first case, the sole real interest is the subject taught and therefore there will be nothing in the horoscope to suggest a specific interest in teaching. However, an interest in history, mathematics, or languages, for example, can frequently be utilized professionally only through teaching, and the horoscope will describe only the interest in these subjects, simply because specific ability for teaching will most likely be quite lacking. In such cases one must be content with inferring the vocational probabilities from the particular interests themselves.

Purely pedagogical interests are shown by a prominence of the signs Leo and Scorpio, and the Ascendant or the dominant planet is usually placed in one of these signs. The tradition that there should be planets in the fifth house does not hold up as well as might be expected, although it is true that Mercury or Jupiter in the fifth house in combination with the right overall pattern may imply interests in education and teaching. Planets are found in the third house with at least the same frequency as in the fifth, in which case it seems likely that the particular intellectual interests shown by the third house planets led the individual into the field of teaching, without there being any essential interest in the educational process itself. Similarly I find that an emphasis on Virgo is frequent in these horoscopes, indicating the tendency to collect, collate, and transmit knowledge rather than any concern for the education and development of the young. It appears that a strong connection between Mercury and Mars is helpful in this transmission of knowledge, and it does not seem to be important here whether the aspect is favorable or unfavorable. Or it is allowable that Mercury and Mars both be strongly placed but without mutual aspect. Finally, Mercury may be in Scorpio and strongly placed.

An unfavorable configuration in the fifth house will not necessarily preclude a teaching career and, as usual, a consideration of the horoscope as a whole is more revealing than any single indication taken by itself. It ought to be remembered that many individuals who have made mistakes at some time in their careers because of impulsiveness or excess of emotion may in the end accomplish a great deal more than the one who has made no mistakes but can establish no kind of relationship with young people because of a lack of warmth and enthusiasm. Naturally, in such cases there must be other more favorable indications at hand that can compensate for the unfortunate fifth house placement and keep it somewhat in check.

It seems to be true that certain unfavorable traits, occurring in a personality otherwise basically harmonious and capable of positive achievement, can assist in strengthening the urge for self-perfection, and that the struggle with one's shortcomings leads to a better understanding of the problems of others. The rather harmonious passivity one finds in persons whose horoscopes show nothing but favorable configurations is not good for the true educator. Teaching should be avoided only in those situations where the fifth house is clearly evil, and as a result there is no sympathy with youth and its playfulness. Living with young people will also prove to be an unpleasant experience, and in extreme cases there can be misfortune involving erotic desires or an unwholesome desire for power. A favorable Saturn in the fifth house is not at all bad for teaching, but it gives greater understanding for an older age group and less for children. Similarly, an unfavorable Mars will only indicate occasional mistakes and will not adversely affect the overall prospects, provided that the personality as a whole is stable.

The trust that a successful educator must have and that is earned through his fairness and broad-mindedness is indicated by a strong Jupiter. The teacher of the specialized subject, who is primarily a transmitter of knowledge, does not necessarily require such an outstanding Jupiter. My experience shows, however, that such a Jupiter is typical of the true educator.

For a teacher who knows something of astrology, a consideration of the transits in both his horoscope and the horoscopes of his students can give hints on the best ways and means to deal with whatever crisis may arise. The teacher can more easily evaluate whether the difficulties encountered are the result of his own method of handling his students or whether they are the result of some critical development in the pupil. He will also more readily understand the physical or personality disturbances that may be taking place, and thereby be of greater help to his pupils.

Example 1: Teacher, September 13, 1876, 11:40 a.m., 53N, 0E35

10th 16 ♍	☉ 21 ♍	♃ 26 ♏ 30
11th 15 ♎	☽ 21 ♋	♂ 10 ♍ 30
12th 6 ♏	♆ 5 ♉	♀ 5 ♌
1st 22 ♏	♅ 22 ♌	☿ 17 ♎
2nd 23 ♐	♄ 3 ♓ 30	
3rd 5 ♒		

Scorpio rising suggests the possibility of an interest in teaching. Mars in the intellectual sign Virgo is just before the cusp of the tenth house and shows energy expended in the pursuit of intellectual accomplishment, especially so as the Sun is in Virgo in the tenth house and sextile the Ascendant. Jupiter gains strength through its location in the first house, and its sextile to the Sun and trine to the Moon reveal a sense of justice, benevolence, and concern for others, all of which are invaluable for the teacher. The Sun and Mars in Virgo in the tenth—or close to its cusp—give the requisite knowledge and the ability to exhaust a subject, as well as

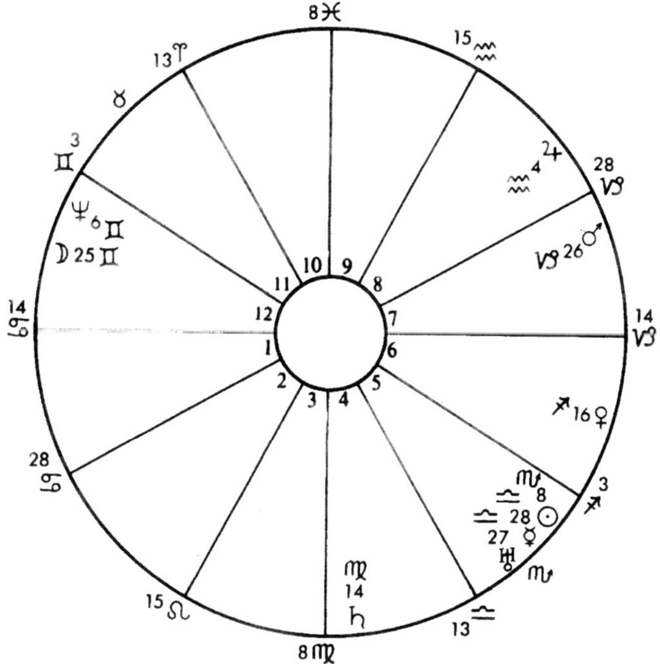

Example 2, Teacher

systematic analysis and conscientiousness. Mercury sextile Uranus in the tenth house is a sign of originality and independence of thought, which will be of assistance in a teaching career. This horoscope is an example of exceptional teaching ability as well as extreme conscientiousness (two dominant planets in Virgo). Despite much physical illness (Ascendant square Uranus, Neptune in the sixth), she is devoted to her profession.

Example 2: Teacher, October 31, 1890, 8:00 p.m., 53N, 0E34

The Sun in Scorpio is in the fifth house (teaching) trine the Ascendant and Midheaven, showing a sincere commitment to the educational field. The Sun is sextile Saturn, the strongest planet in the horoscope, and is therefore strong in terms of general as well as individual structure. The sextile of the Sun and Saturn denotes considerable stability and self-discipline, and inclines to an expression of these traits in intellectual terms, as Saturn is strongly placed in the fourth house in Virgo. Mercury conjunct Uranus in the fifth house, and square Mars as well, shows independence of thought in teaching, and an exceptional talent for the transmission of knowledge. This is clearly a horoscope of superior teaching ability.

Example 3: Teacher, February 20, 1892, 11:30 p.m., 53N, 0E53

10th 20 ♌	☉ 1 ♓ 49	♃ 24 ♓
11th 23 ♍	☽ 1 ♐ 15	♂ 17 ♐
12th 17 ♎	♆ 6 ♊	♀ 8 ♈
1st 6 ♏	♅ 6 ♏	☿ 20 ♒ 30
2nd 3 ♐	♄ 29 ♍	
3rd 10 ♑		

Scorpio again rises, while Mercury is the second strongest planet in the horoscope and is sextile Mars, indicating good self-expression and a talent for teaching. Mercury in Aquarius, according to my own statistics, denotes a lively intellect and is frequently found in the horoscopes of teachers. Jupiter and Venus receive quite favorable aspects in the fifth house and augur well for a good personal relationship with youngsters.

Example 4: Assistant master at a gymnasium, teacher of modern languages, August 8,1884, 4:00 a.m., 51N, 0E49

10th 18 ♈	☉ 16 ♌	♃ 16 ♌
11th 29 ♉	☽ 29 ♒ 50	♂ 7 ♎
12th 9 ♋	♆ 23 ♉	♀ 12 ♋
1st 10 ♌	♅ 26 ♍	☿ 8 ♍ 30

2nd 26 ♌ ♄ 21 ♊
3rd 18 ♍

Leo rises, and the Sun and Jupiter are conjunct in Leo in the first house, signifying stability, perseverance, authority, and a strong sense of justice, cooperation, and trustworthiness. Saturn in the eleventh house is sextile the Sun and Jupiter, indicating considerable self-discipline, and these traits will be conspicuous in the professional life as Saturn is sextile the Midheaven and the Sun and Jupiter are trine this angle. Mars sextile the Ascendant shows that there will be no lack of energy and drive when these are required. The love of knowledge is shown by Mercury and Uranus in Virgo, but despite the strength of these planets, they are not dominant and must be considered secondary to the purely pedagogical interests, as these Virgo planets have no essential relationship with the angular houses. This teacher has developed quite a few practical and theoretical innovations in the educational field.

The Linguist

The spontaneous knack for picking up foreign languages is generally a result of a prominence of the air signs in the horoscope, and primarily of Libra and Gemini. The air signs produce a more active or sanguine temperament, and they possess a strong urge to put their feelings into words, with the result that their contact with the environment is more verbal and immediate. This predisposition makes it easier for them to pick up and absorb the unfamiliar sounds of a foreign language than would be possible for a person whose horoscope, for example, showed a predominance of the earth signs, which incline to a melancholic temperament and a certain taciturnity. However, the air signs do not have much sense of the laws of syntax and grammar; they learn languages more through a sensitive receptivity than by an understanding of grammatical relationships.

The other Mercury sign—Virgo—is much more interested in the formal study of grammar and in linguistics. But they have difficulty in actually speaking a foreign language, and this is a problem that can only be overcome by a very strong Mercury, and if possible a Mercury-Moon aspect in the horoscope. A strong Mercury is indispensable for the linguist. Therefore, the ideal horoscope for the linguist would be one with the Ascendant in Virgo and important planets placed in Gemini so that a feeling for grammar and syntax would be combined with the facility for picking up the rhythm, intonation, etc. of the spoken language. A strong Mercury would also be necessary.

Example 1: Male, May 27, 1894, 11:15 a.m., 49N, 24E

10th 5 ♊	☉ 6 ♊	♃ 12 ♊
11th 12 ♋	☽ 2 ♓	♂ 12 ♓
12th 14 ♌	♆ 13 ♊	♀ 22 ♈ 30
1st 10 ♍	♅ 12 ♏ 30	☿ 14 ♊ 30
2nd 2 ♎	♄ 19 ♎	
3rd 1 ♏		

The Gemini planets show the natural gift for picking up languages and the adaptability of the ear to foreign sounds. The Virgo Ascendant provides support through its facility in the comprehension of grammar. This is not the horoscope of a scholar in the field of linguistics, but of a capable businessman, which is implied by the Sun and Jupiter in the tenth house trine Saturn in the second house. As these planets are the strongest in the horoscope, they supersede Mercury in importance. (When Mercury occurs in the tenth house, the tendency, as we have seen, is to the expression of the more practical side of its nature, rather than the intellectual.) This man speaks several languages fluently and also has a lively interest in the study of grammar.

Example 2: Female, March 28, 1900, 5:30 p.m., Manchester

10th 26 ♊	☉ 7 ♈ 36	♃ 11 ♐
11th 3 ♌	☽ 7 ♓	♂ 22 ♓

12th 3 ♍   ♆ 24 ♊   ♀ 20 ♉ 30
1st 27 ♍   ♅ 12 ♐ 30   ☿ 1 ♈
2nd 20 ♎   ♄ 5 ♑
3rd 19 ♏

Mercury on the cusp of the seventh house must be considered the dominant planet, and with Virgo rising indicates the possibility of a talent for languages. This lady speaks several languages with considerable fluency.

Example 3. Female, June 15, 1888, 12:30 p.m., 52N30, 13E23

10th 1 ♋   ☉ 24 ♊ 44   ♃ 28 ♏ 37
11th 7 ♌   ☽ 2 ♍ 10   ♂ 15 ♎ 23
12th 7 ♍   ♆ 0 ♊ 43   ♀ 17 ♊ 30
1st 1 ♎   ♅ 13 ♎ 08   ☿ 18 ♋ 45
2nd 25 ♎   ♄ 4 ♌ 17
3rd 25 ♏

The air signs are heavily tenanted and confer an easy, rather unconscious facility for picking up foreign languages. This lady speaks almost all the European languages.

The Cleric

Only Protestant clergymen are considered in this evaluation. The horoscopes of members of the Catholic clergy appear to be quite different, and it can be supposed that a quite different mentality is to be found among them.

The basis of all spiritual activity is faith, and those people of a negative or doubting temperament could clearly obtain no satisfaction in the clergy. (The structure of the horoscope as a whole must show this faith, and although it is possible that traits of doubt and criticism can appear, they should not be dominant.) So we find that the fire signs are predominant in the horoscopes of Protestant clergymen, a sign of aggressive faith in an ideal, while the earth signs are not much represented. Those born under the fire signs are able to give easy expression to their feelings and ideas. Most frequently one finds Leo or Sagittarius on the Ascendant, but it may be surmised that the low incidence of Aries is because of the short duration of its rising in northern latitudes. Except for the sign Leo, the fall and winter signs are most frequently rising, and the sign Capricorn in particular seems to rise more frequently than would normally be expected.

The Sun is frequently in the fire signs, and in particular, Aries. Apparently the leadership traits represented by Aries are well suited to the clergy.

The Moon is frequently in Leo or Aries, again indicating the authoritative traits commonly found among the clergy. Virgo is most represented next, probably signifying the clergyman-author. The Moon appears most frequently in the third and ninth houses, which is a feature of the horoscopes of writers and poets as well. It appears that one can distinguish two kinds of clergy: the one with planets in the third house will demonstrate a greater interest in the pursuit of learning, while the one with planets in the ninth house will be impelled by religious motives to construct a suitable ideology or Weltanschauung. Incidentally; the writer or poet who reveals a religious temperament will also have a strong ninth house. The meaning of individual planetary positions I am not able to give as the material now at hand is insufficient for any meaningful evaluation, but it is striking how many horoscopes of both Protestant and Catholic clergy have Mars in Taurus.

An assumption based on tradition is that a strong Jupiter should appear in the horoscope of the clergy, but this does not always seem to be the case; although, aspects between the Sun and Jupiter are very frequent in the horoscopes of strongly religious persons. According to tradition, aspects between Mars and Jupiter are also characteristic of the horoscopes of clergymen, and although these are found they do not appear to be the most significant component, or at any rate, this vocation is not by any means exclusively shown by Jupiter-Mars contacts. Jupiter is usually strong, and is often in an angular house or in aspect to an angular house cusp, but Mars is usually relatively weak and is at best only found in the fourth house where its energy is more introverted. The vocation of clergyman, it seems, is more to be seen through a consideration of the personality as a whole; that is, through the horoscope's structure rather than through the recognition of specific talents that result from clearly dominant planets.

If Neptune is strong there will be an added note of mysticism. One final observation is that planets are usually found in the first three quadrants—from the first house through the ninth—and rarely in the fourth quadrant, the most positive.

Example 1: Clergyman, March 19, 1885, 1:20 p.m., 51N20, 0E49

The Ascendant is in Leo. The Sun is crossing from Pisces to Aries and conjunct Mercury in Aries and both planets are in the ninth house and in aspect to the Ascendant. This man's beliefs will be expressed with assertion and self-will, and there is a talent for oratory.

Example 2: Clergyman, March 7, 1868, 2:00 a.m., 51N45, 12E23

10th 16 ♎	☉ 16 ♓ 47	♃ 19 ♓ 30
11th 11 ♏	☽ 22 ♌	♂ 2 ♓
12th 29 ♏	♆ 14 ♈	♀ 24 ♈ 30
1st 14 ♐	♅ 9 ♋	☿ 19 ♓ 30
2nd 24 ♑	♄ 5 ♐ 30	
3rd 10 ♓		

The Ascendant is in the fire sign Sagittarius, and the Moon—as is so frequently the case—is in Leo. The Sun is in Pisces in the third house in conjunction with Mercury and Jupiter. Neptune on the cusp of the fourth house indicates mysticism and great sensitivity. Jupiter is stronger than would at first appear through its square to

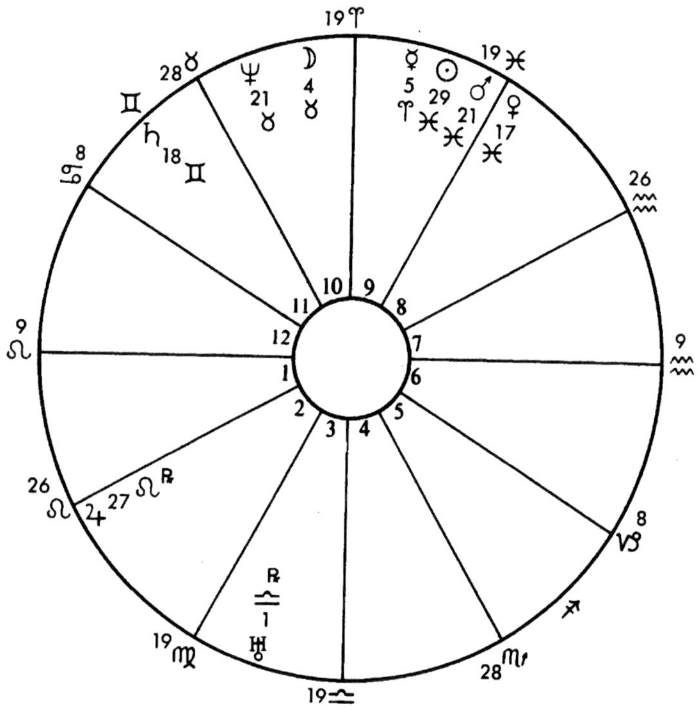

Example 2, Clergyman

the Ascendant and conjunction with the Sun and Mercury. The fourth quadrant has only one planet.

Example 3: Clergyman, September 28, 1899, 2:15 a.m., Nuremberg

10th 9 ♉	☉ 4 ♎ 4	♃ 11 ♏
11th 18 ♊	☽ 20 ♋ 30	♂ 4 ♏ 30
12th 24 ♋	♆ 27 ♊	♀ 7 ♎ 45
1st 21 ♌	♅ 5 ♐	☿ 2 ♎
2nd 10 ♍	♄ 18 ♐	
3rd 5 ♎		

The Ascendant is in Leo, and the Sun and Mercury are in Libra in the third house. The conjunction of Jupiter and Mars in the fourth house is the strongest configuration in the horoscope. The fourth quadrant contains only the Moon and Neptune.

Example 4: Clergyman, July 17, 1863, 7:00 a.m., 52N18, 0E36

10th 13 ♉	☉ 24 ♋	♃ 19 ♎
11th 22 ♊	☽ 8 ♌	♂ 20 ♌
12th 27 ♋	♆ 6 ♈	♀ 9 ♍ 30
1st 25 ♌	♅ 23 ♊	☿ 7 ♋
2nd 15 ♍	♄ 0 ♎ 30	
3rd 10 ♎		

The Ascendant, Moon, and Mars are in the fire sign Leo, and Jupiter is in the third house. This is the horoscope of a much-loved pastor.

Example 5: Clergyman, May 22, 1881, 9:45 p.m., 51N20, 0E49

The Ascendant, Moon and Mars are all in the fire signs Sagittarius or Aries. The Moon and Mars are in the third house. Jupiter is strong in the fourth house and is sextile Mars. Mercury is sextile Mars, and the Moon enhances the talent for oratory.

Example 6: Clergyman, July 29, 1880, 7:00 p.m., 51N20, 0E49

The Sun, Venus and Mercury are in the fire sign Leo in the seventh house, so this group is the most significant feature of the horoscope. The strong Mercury shows the talent for oratory. Jupiter in Aries gains strength because of its exact square to the Ascendant. As is frequent in such horoscopes, the Moon is in the third house. The fourth quadrant is untenanted.

Example 7: Clergyman, July 31, 1889, 5:00 p.m., 51N20, 0E40

The Ascendant, Sun, Mercury, Jupiter and Saturn are in fire signs, while Jupiter in the first house is the most powerful planet. The

Moon and Uranus are in Virgo in the ninth house. Mercury conjunct Mars confers oratory. The fourth quadrant is untenanted.

Example 8: Clergyman, April 14, 1878, 11:10 a.m., 51N20, 0E49

The Ascendant and the Sun are in fire signs, and Jupiter on the cusp of the first house is the dominant planet. The Moon is in Virgo in the third house, while Venus and Saturn are in the ninth house.

Example 9: Clergyman, March 27, 1878, 2:15 a.m., 51N20, 0E49

The winter sign Capricorn rises, and the Sun and Mercury are in the third house in the fire sign Aries. Jupiter is very strongly placed in the first house, and its trine to Mars increases enthusiasm and inspiration. Mercury is sextile Mars, showing the oratorical ability. The fourth quadrant is untenanted.

Example 10: Clergyman, June 10, 1869, 9:00 p.m., 51N20, 0E49

The winter sign Capricorn rises. Jupiter is well-placed in the fourth house and its conjunction with the very powerful Mercury indicates oratorical ability. The trine of Jupiter and Mars compensates for the lack of planets in the fire signs, and increases enthusiasm and inspiration. The fourth quadrant is weak, containing only Saturn in the twelfth house.

Example 11: Clergyman, December 18, 1893, 8:30 p.m., 51N20, 0E49

The Ascendant, Sun, Moon and Mercury are in fire signs. Jupiter is very powerful in the tenth house, and gains additional strength through its square to the Ascendant. The Moon is in the ninth house while Saturn is in the third. The fourth quadrant is rather weakly represented as only Jupiter and Neptune are therein.

The Fine Arts

During our study of the vocations in the natural sciences and in liberal arts we found a prominent Mercury, albeit with many possible variations, to be a constant factor because intellectual power is essential to work of that nature. Similarly, we found that vocations in the fine arts demand a prominent Venus, which represents the more sensitive perceptive faculties that are necessary for the artist. According to one manual, Venus rules the following vocations: musician, artist, jeweler, dealers in silks and draperies, books, toys, perfumes. Further: restauranteurs, cooks, tenant farmers. But the traditional concept of a Venus profession leaves us with much too wide a choice and the fact is that other configurations are also required to produce the artist and they determine the particular way the power of Venus will be expressed. It should be noted that it is often much easier to recognize in the horoscope the basic artistic predisposition of the personality than it is to determine the precise area of artistic talent—there are borderline cases where the exact determination of such an area is quite difficult.

It is wise to be very cautious when Venus is found in Aries or Capricorn, and at the same time is the dominant planet, as these signs are unfavorable for the satisfactory development of the necessary range of feeling response, or they indicate a strong intellectual tendency combined with such response.

The Writer

The talent for writing above all demands the capacity to comprehend and organize diverse material and then give to it an esthetic expression. Accordingly, one will find a very strong Venus in the horoscope of writers and poets, but as writing also demands constant intellectual evaluation, reflection, and an understanding of widely varying social milieus and possibilities within human nature, one must also expect to find a prominent Mercury. Actually, Venus and Mercury are almost always well placed, and quite often in aspect to each other. Mercury is frequently in aspect with the Ascendant, Midheaven, or planet in an angular house. Mercury in the first or tenth house is rare and in fact is possible only with other quite specific configurations such as an aspect with Venus. In such cases it is usually found that Mercury is actually several degrees *before* the degree on the cusp of the first or tenth house, thereby lending a more intellectual form of expression to the Mercury function. (My experience is that it is important that Mercury not be in the first or tenth house and at the same time be the most powerful planet; that is, in exact conjunction with the cusp of the first or tenth house. A simultaneous aspect to Venus would provide the only possible exception to this rule. The further away Mercury lies from the cusp, and particularly if in the next sign from that on the cusp, the more is dissipated the active and extraverted side of its nature, which is more or less inimical to writing.) Mercury is more frequently found in the seventh or fourth house. However, these conditions do not apply to Venus as the increase in sensuousness indicated by that planet's location in the first or tenth house is by no means inimical to creative activity, but instead gives increased vividness, richness, and vitality.

The relative strength of the esthetic and the intellectual in a given writer's work will be reflected in whether Venus or Mercury is the more powerful planet by position in an angular house, aspect to an angular cusp, or aspect to the dominant planet. When in aspect to a dominant planet located in the first house, the influence of Venus or Mercury is strongly established as a basic underlying personality factor rather than the indicator of any specific talent.

The love of knowledge usually found among writers is seen by planets in the third or ninth house, and Mercury or Venus are particularly well placed in either of these houses. In the ninth house there is a greater tendency to establish in the artistic work a comprehensive point of view, while in the third house the tendency is for a narrower and more analytical approach. Planets in the fourth house may confer an uncanny insight into the nature of people and surroundings.

It is unfair to ascribe superior talent to any one of the twelve signs as each can produce an author or artist; but each sign does have a characteristic manifestation. For example, Leo symbolizes the broad dramatic narrative, combining elements of poetry and realism. Virgo is reflective and inclined to a more intellectual and frequently critical handling of the material. Sagittarius produces lyricism and a love of nature, while Libra confers dramatic talent and a sharp esthetic sense. Gemini gives esprit, elegance, intellect, and a sense of style. It cannot be denied that Virgo and Gemini on the Ascendant—or prominent through planetary placements—may facilitate to a greater degree a talent for writing. But when considering any individual case this broad generality is of not much use.

Poetry consists of more distilled and intense forms of expression and astrologically seems to require a greater inner tension that can only be described as inharmonious. For this reason it happens that in the horoscopes of poets we find an opposition between the Sun and Moon, indicating the conflict between unconscious, uncontrolled drives and the conscious urge to understand and to formulate expression. This conflict is discharged and neutralized by the creative act. Moreover, it should not be assumed that the horoscopes of writers will show a predominance of fortunate aspects. Some suffering is always involved in the development of the capacity to comprehend in depth and express with universal meaning the nature of one's personal feelings and conflicts. These conflicts are reflected in disharmonious aspects, while appropriate favorable aspects conjoined to them grant the possibility of their creative expression. Or stated another way, it frequently happens that critical aspects to the artistic configuration add depth to ability, and the creative act can be seen as an overcompensation for inner failings and insoluble conflicts. Where there are no such critical aspects, one may find talent, but the works produced will be insipid and deprived of depth. On the other hand, if the critical aspects predominate, the creative work will reveal disharmony and lack of unity and control. Though profound and significant, the

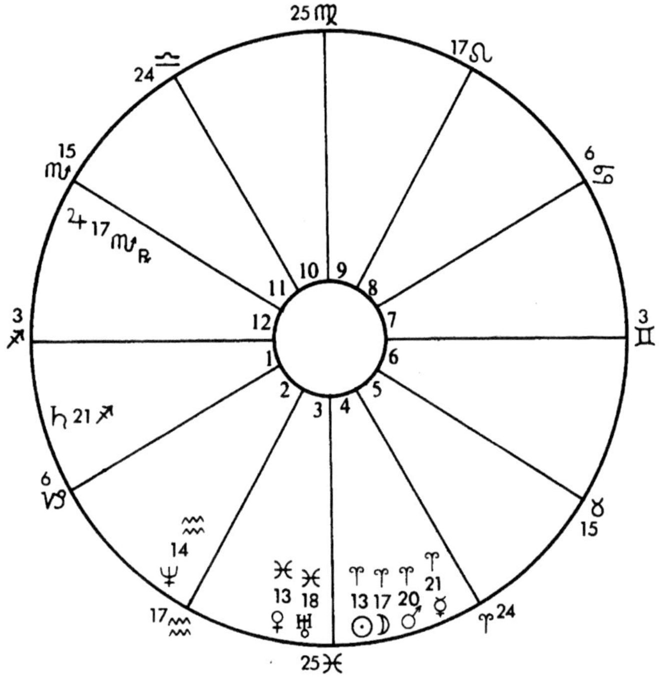

Example 1, Emile Zola

greatest representation of an artistic ideal will not have been achieved.

Poetic talent is shown by a strong Neptune, and particularly by the aspects of Neptune to the Sun, or by Neptune in the ninth house.

Example 1: Emile Zola, April 2, 1840, 11:00 p.m., Paris

Sagittarius rises, and Saturn in the first house is the dominant planet, in aspect to seven planets: Neptune, Venus, Uranus, Sun, Moon, Mars, and Mercury. Writing ability is shown by the trine between this first-house Saturn and Mercury, which in turn has several aspects, showing an unusually active and versatile intel-

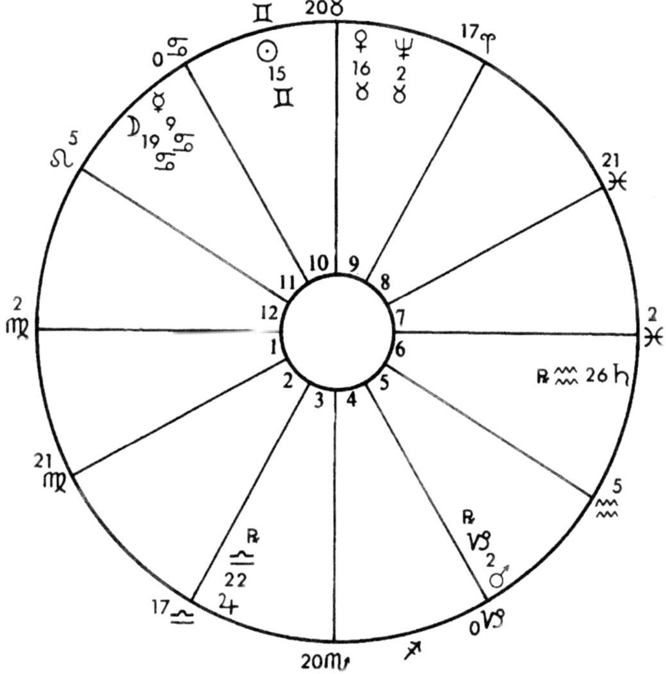

Example 2, Thomas Mann

lect. However, Mercury conjunct Mars in Aries will lead to hyperactivity and stress. As is frequent with writers, Venus is in the third house, and its square to Saturn in the first house and its conjunction with Uranus reveal a disharmonious and even unstable emotional makeup. However, the dominant Saturn adequately expresses Zola's gloomy and dour personality. Poetic talent is shown by the aspects of Neptune to Saturn, the Sun and Moon.

Example 2: Thomas Mann, June 6, 1875, 10:15 a.m., Lubeck

In this horoscope Venus is the strongest planet and is posited in the ninth house, but just *before* the tenth house cusp. It indicates, despite the versatile and penetrating intellect shown by Virgo rising and the Sun in Gemini, as well as the sextile of Mercury to Venus, that the esthetic temperament takes precedence. Jupiter in Libra in the third house in good aspect to the tenth house Sun increases the creative drive and confers an understanding of vast social interrelationships.

Example 3: Otto Julius Bierbaum, June 28, 1865, 8:30 a.m., Grunberg in Schl

10th 16 ♉	☉ 6 ♋ 30	♃ 22 ♐ 30
11th 25 ♊	☽ 6 ♍	♂ 20 ♌ 30
12th 29 ♋	♆ 10 ♈ 30	♀ 22 ♉ 30
1st 27 ♌	♅ 0 ♋	☿ 2 ♋
2nd 17 ♍	♄ 23 ♎ 36	
3rd 12 ♎		

Venus rules the horoscope in the tenth house and in its own sign Taurus. Clearly the horoscope is an artistic one and conducive to the expression of the feelings. The square of Venus to Mars gives wit, humor, and a certain frivolity, but also some conflict resulting from traits of sensuality. Mercury in the eleventh house is in close conjunction with the Sun and Uranus and also sextile the Ascendant, indicating an original intellect. The Moon in Virgo in the first house in aspect with Mercury also shows a good intellect (though still of secondary importance in the horoscope) but one that is *subjective* in nature, which results from the close conjunction of Mercury with the Sun.

Following are brief notes on the horoscopes of various writers. Only the essential configurations are given.

Example 4: Alfred Mombert. Mercury and the Moon are conjunct Venus in the third house.

Example 5: Wilhelm von Scholz. Mercury conjunct Uranus in the seventh house and in opposition to Saturn in the first is the strongest planet in the horoscope.

Example 6: Joseph Ponten. Mercury is conjunct the Sun in Gemini in the ninth house, and the Sun is trine the Ascendant. Venus is sextile the Midheaven, trine Uranus, and in aspect to the Moon and Neptune.

Example 7: Hermann Hesse. Mercury is on the cusp of the seventh house, trine the Midheaven, and in opposition to the dominant planet in the first house.

Example 8: Georg Trakel. Venus is conjunct Mars in the ninth house. Mercury is relatively weak, but receives several aspects.

Example 9: Gustav Falke. Venus and Mercury are in the third house in aspect with Moon and Uranus. Jupiter is also in the third.

Example 10: Peter Hille. Venus in the first house is the most powerful planet. Mercury is closely conjunct the Virgo Sun in the second house and trine Uranus and the Moon in the tenth. This Moon-Uranus configuration denotes the Bohemian. and shows marked eccentricity in one's private life and conduct.

Example 11: Johannes Schlaf. Mercury rising is the strongest planet, is sextile Venus, and receives several other aspects.

Example 12: Stephan George. Venus is conjunct Mercury in the ninth house and trine to Saturn in the first house. Saturn is the horoscope's strongest planet. (Note the similarity with Zola, R. Huch, Hesse, and v. Scholz).

Example 13: Theodor Daubler. Mercury is in Virgo and conjunct the Ascendant, but just before the rising degree. Venus is sextile the Ascendant, and Jupiter is in the third house in trine to the conjunction of the Moon and Venus.

Example 14: Hugo von Hoffmannsthal. Mercury is conjunct Saturn, Venus, and the Sun in Aquarius in the second house, and all these planets are sextile the Ascendant and trine the Midheaven.

Example 15: Rainer Maria Rilke. Mercury is the strongest planet and is conjunct the fourth house cusp and receives several aspects. Venus is also strong in the fourth house and receives several aspects.

Example 16: Georg Kaiser. Venus is conjunct the Sun in Sagittarius in the third house and is sextile the Ascendant. The Moon is conjunct Mercury in the third house.

Example 17: Gustav Meyrink. Venus in the tenth house is the strongest planet and is trine the Gemini Ascendant. The Sun is conjunct Mercury and Mars in the ninth house.

Example 18: Frank Wedekind. Venus in the tenth house is the strongest planet and is conjunct the Sun and Mercury. Uranus in the ninth house is trine the Ascendant.

Example 19: Heinrich von Kleist, October 18, 1777, 1:00 a.m., Frankfurt an der Oder. The rising degree in Leo forms an exact sextile to the Sun and Mercury in the artistic sign Libra in the third house.

Example 20: Jakob Wasserman, March 10, 1873, 11:15 a.m., Furth in Bavaria. Venus is stronger here than Mercury because of its sextile to the Ascendant and Midheaven, although the latter is very strong through its square to the Ascendant. The position of the Moon and Jupiter point to writing. The Sun in Pisces in the tenth house is not exactly weak, but its lack of aspects to the angular cusps places it third in importance in the horoscope. As an element of general structure this position influences the basic personality by granting compassion and sympathy.

The Painter

The talent for painting is much more clearly a matter of feeling than of intellect. Accordingly, a powerful Venus and a predominance of the Venus signs Taurus and Libra is to be expected; Libra is more commonly found. For example, in the statistics compiled by Moufang and Klockler, the Sun was by far most frequently found in the sign Libra. A feeling for color—clearly indispensable for the painter—is always increased through Venus-Jupiter aspects, or in the relative prominence of both these planets in the horoscope. The sign Sagittarius rising, or otherwise emphasized, gives a talent for painting with perhaps a preference for landscapes, which results from the love of nature characteristic of Sagittarius. This sign can also compensate for a weak Jupiter. A powerful Moon, or the sign Cancer prominent, confers a good sense of form. The conjunction of the Sun and Venus occurs very frequently and can replace the Libra factor, or enhance it, should it already be important.

Example 1: Max Liebermann, July 20, 1847, 8:00 a.m., Berlin

Venus in the first house (see page 62) is the most powerful planet; its sextile to Jupiter is of course the painter aspect. Jupiter gains strength through its exact sextile to the rising degree. Venus in the earth sign Virgo denotes objectivity and a tendency to naturalism—the more so by its opposition to Saturn. The good sense of form is seen in the emphasis on Cancer.

Example 2: Painter and illustrator, October 20, 1891, 3:00 p.m., 51N31, 0E48

10th 15 ♐	☉ 26 ♎	♃ 8 ♓ 30
11th 2 ♑	☽ 8 ♊	♂ 29 ♍
12th 21 ♑	♆ 9 ♊	♀ 5 ♏
1st 23 ♒	♅ 1 ♏ 30	☿ 22 ♎
2nd 23 ♈	♄ 25 ♍	
3rd 25 ♉		

The ascending degree is in Aquarius and trine to the conjunction of Mercury and the Sun in Libra. This position of the Sun in the sign of painting is important. Jupiter is in the first house trine Venus, so that the two painting configurations—the Sun in Libra and Venus trine Jupiter—are clearly the most significant for this horoscope.

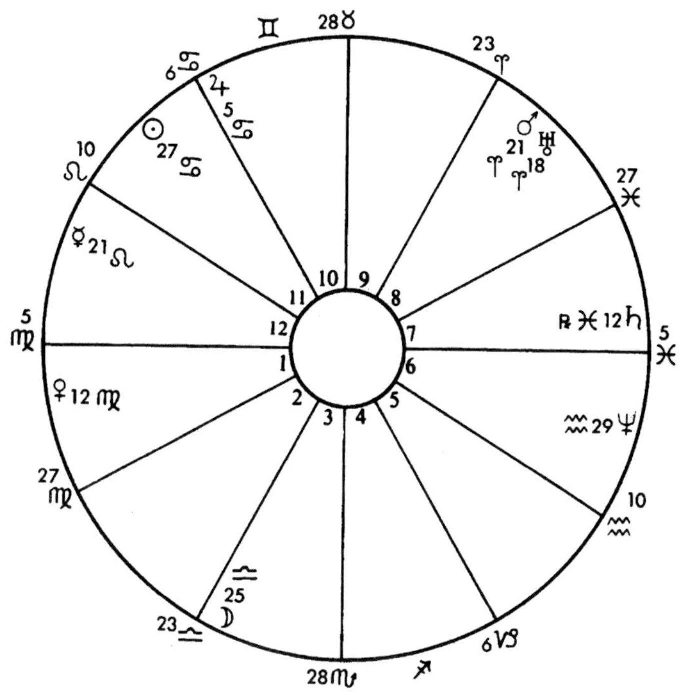

Example 1, Max Liebermann

Example 3: Hans Thoma, October 2, 1839, 11:40 p.m., Bernau

10th 3 ♈	☉ 9 ♎	♃ 25 ♎
11th 10 ♉	☽ 16 ♌ 30	♂ 0 ♐
12th 22 ♊	♆ 10 ♒	♀ 14 ♎
1st 26 ♋	♅ 13 ♓	☿ 29 ♍
2nd 13 ♌	♄ 6 ♐	
3rd 4 ♍		

The Sun and Venus in conjunction in Libra in the fourth house dominate the horoscope. Jupiter in Libra in the fourth house is

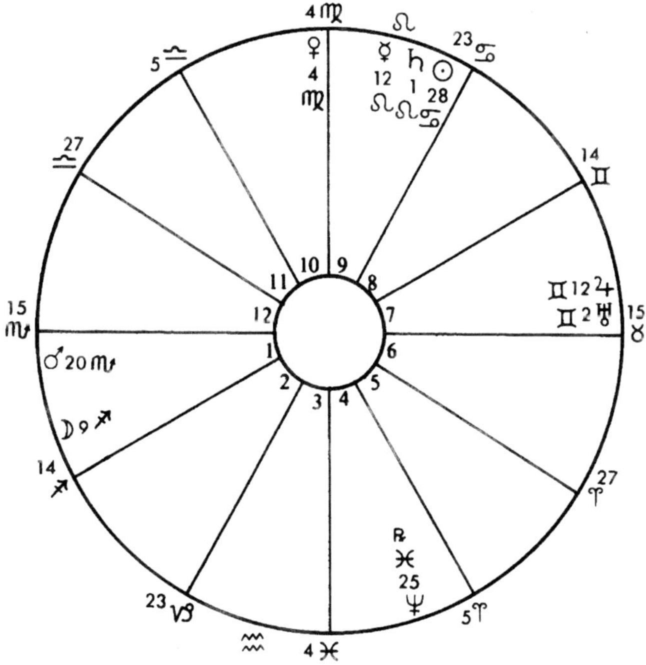

Example 4, Lovis Corinth

powerful, both by its rather wide conjunction with Venus and its exact square to the Ascendant. Cancer rising gives the sense of form. Mercury aspecting both Mars and the Ascendant shows the talent for drawing and sketching.

Example 4: Lovis Corinth, July 21, 1858, 2:00 p.m., Tapiau, East Prussia

Venus rules the horoscope on the cusp of the tenth house and is square Jupiter as well, so that painting ability is clearly shown. Mars in Scorpio in the first house shows a passionate nature that will surely be evident in the creative work. The aspect of Mars to

Mercury shows a talent for drawing and sketching, but as they are in square, there is indication that some inhibition or limitation will present difficulties and must be overcome.

Example 5: Heinrich Zille, January 10, 1858, 5:00 p.m., Radeburg near Dresden

10th 6 ♈	☉ 20 ♑	♃ 6 ♉ 10
11th 15 ♉	☽ 29 ♏ 56	♂ 1 ♏ 16
12th 27 ♊	♆ 20 ♓ 20	♀ 8 ♑ 30
1st 0 ♌	♅ 25 ♉ 30	☿ 0 ♒ 10
2nd 17 ♌	♄ 25 ♋ 17	
3rd 8 ♍		

As might be expected, Mercury, and not Venus, rules the horoscope of this illustrator. Mercury receives bad aspects which are a sign not of his virtuoso technique, but rather his struggle with the materials of his art and the resulting achievement. Zille's milieu is clearly shown by Saturn close to the Ascendant, and the planets in the sixth house show his interest in the proletariat, their needs and their poverty. Venus in the sixth house is square the Midheaven and trine Jupiter in the tenth, so that the painting aspect is found in this horoscope as well.

The Sculptor

There are very few horoscopes of sculptors available and for the present a detailed evaluation cannot be given. My experience shows that, in contrast with the painters, the Sun and Moon are frequently found in Scorpio, and aspects between Mars and the Sun or Moon are very frequent. It would seem from this that sculpture is a Mars-related art. The eastern half of the horoscope is usually heavily tenanted, and indicates strong academic tendencies in the artistic work. Venus, by contrast, can be relatively weak. Beyond this, nothing is established with any certainty.

Example 1: Sculptor, August 3,1876, 4:00 a.m., 51N, 0E56

10th 8 ♈	☉ 11 ♌ 03	♃ 22 ♏ 28
11th 22 ♉	☽ 17 ♑ 25	♂ 14 ♌ 10
12th 3 ♋	♆ 5 ♉	♀ 14 ♋
1st 4 ♌	♅ 20 ♌	☿ 9 ♌
2nd 22 ♌	♄ 6 ♓	
3rd 13 ♍		

The Ascendant is in the fire sign Leo and the first house Sun is in aspect to Mars and Uranus. This is the horoscope of a well-known and popular sculptor who has also done much fine handiwork, particularly jewelry. Tradition has it that the goldsmith is ruled by the sign Leo.

Example 2: Sculptress, October 30,1905, 5:00 a.m., 47N33, 0E30

10th 14 ♋	☉ 6 ♏	♃ 4 ♊ 30
11th 19 ♌	☽ 3 ♐	♂ 16 ♑
12th 18 ♍	♆ 10 ♋ 30	♀ 10 ♎ 30
1st 11 ♎	♅ 1 ♑	☿ 17 ♏
2nd 7 ♏	♄ 26 ♒	
3rd 8 ♐		

Libra rising and Venus on the Ascendant immediately suggest an interest in art as well as the probability of a talent for painting. Mars is the second strongest planet in the horoscope, and is located in Capricorn in the fourth house and sextile to the Sun in Scorpio, an aspect frequently found in the charts of sculptors.

Example 3: Sculptor, born March 24, 1884, 11:30 a.m., Berlin

10th 25 ♓	☉ 4 ♈	♃ 24 ♋ 30
11th 3 ♉	☽ 27 ♒	♂ 3 ♌ 30
12th 18 ♊	♆ 19 ♉	♀ 16 ♉ 30

1st 24 ♋	♅ 26 ♍	☿ 28 ♓ 30
2nd 10 ♌	♄ 5 ♊ 30	
3rd 29 ♌		

The Sun is in the Mars sign Aries in the tenth house and trine to Mars in Leo in the first house, which points up the strong Mars influence in the artistic work. The close conjunction of Venus and Neptune is an indication of this artist's considerable musical talent.

Example 4: Sculptor. Venus is weak, and Mars is conjunct Mercury on the cusp of the fourth house rules the horoscope. The Moon is in Scorpio.

Example 5: Sculptor. The Sun and Mercury in Scorpio on the Ascendant rule the horoscope. Mars in the second house exactly trines the Midheaven. Venus is relatively weak in the eleventh house, but receives several aspects.

Example 6: Auguste Rodin, November 12, 1840, noon, Paris

The Sun in Scorpio rules the horoscope and is sextile Mars, which in turn is exactly trine the Ascendant and therefore the second strongest factor. The creative imagination of this great artist is shown by the powerful Jupiter.

Example 7: Max Klinger, February 18, 1857, 1:05 a.m., Leipzig

10th 11 ♍	☉ 29 ♒ 20	♃ 10 ♈
11th 11 ♎	☽ 9 ♐ 27	♂ 27 ♓
12th 4 ♏	♆ 19 ♓	♀ 15 ♈ 30
1st 21 ♏	♅ 21 ♉	☿ 4 ♒
2nd 22 ♐	♄ 7 ♋ 30	
3rd 1 ♒		

Neptune and Mars are strongly placed through their conjunction in the fourth house, trine to the Ascendant and sextile to Uranus. The

Venus-Jupiter conjunction indicates painting. The sextile between Mercury and Mars shows the facility for drawing and sketching.

The Musician

Unfortunately there are no exhaustive studies that might give an adequate statistical picture of the typical musician, and therefore we must rely on the statistics presented in several individual studies and on the many horoscopes I have seen in order to get an idea of what should constitute a musician's horoscope. As in all artists' horoscopes, Venus—the symbol of feeling and sensitivity—is almost always dominant, and placed in an angular house or in aspect to an angular house cusp. Occasionally it is found in the second house and in aspect to the Midheaven or Ascendant or planets in the first or tenth house. Aspects to Neptune are very frequent; moreover, Flambart observed a high frequency of Venus-Uranus aspects, both favorable and unfavorable. However, no special house emphasis has been established, although the seventh house, and perhaps the fifth, may contain important planets, but these positions can by no means be considered typical. The pattern of house emphasis mirrors personality characteristics that have nothing *essential* to do with musical ability, but which may give to that ability a certain direction or color.

Karl Krafft of Zurich, in considering a large amount of data, found the Sun most frequently placed in Libra, and secondly, Taurus. He also found a high number of Venus-Neptune and Moon-Uranus contacts. Schwab of Berlin believes to have established a correlation between musicality and the Moon in Cancer. The most frequent signs on the Ascendant appear to be Taurus, Gemini, Cancer, Virgo, Sagittarius, and perhaps Pisces. When the Sun is found in one of these signs on the Ascendant, or in the first house, some degree of musical ability will be found.

The interpretive musician is easier to recognize than the composer, and many composers—but by no means all—seem to lack the prominent Venus that one would normally expect; unfortunately,

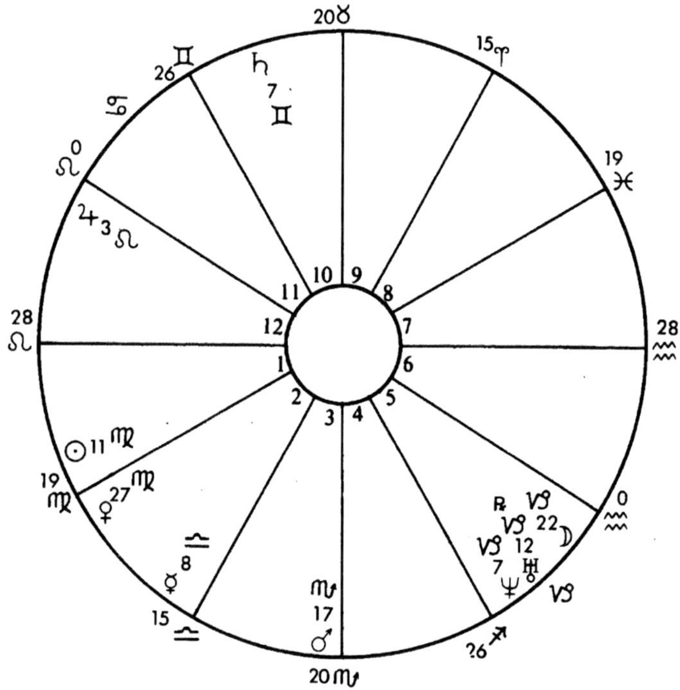

Example 1, Anton Bruckner

there is not enough material at hand to probe further for the possible reasons.

Example 1: Anton Bruckner, September 4, 1824, 4:15 a.m., Ausfelden near Linz

The Sun is in the musical sign Virgo in the first house. Venus in Virgo is in the second house and trine the MC as well as trine Uranus and the Moon.

Example 2: Kurt Thomas, winner of the 1927 Beethoven prize, May 25, 1904, 4:00 a.m., Tonningen on the Eider (Schleswig)

10th 24 ♑	☉ 3 ♊ 30	♃ 20 ♈
11th 17 ♒	☽ 9 ♎ 30	♂ 5 ♊
12th 24 ♓	♆ 4 ♋ 30	♀ 21 ♉ 30
1st 28 ♉	♅ 29 ♐	☿ 17 ♉ 30
2nd 21 ♊	♄ 21 ♒	
3rd 8 ♋		

This horoscope bears a striking resemblance to that of Richard Wagner. The Sun is in the musical sign Gemini, and the Ascendant is in the musical sign Taurus. Venus in Taurus is trine the Midheaven and in weak conjunction with the Ascendant.

Example 3: Paul Hindemith, November 16, 1895, 9:30 p.m., Hanau

Venus is powerful on the IC and sextile Jupiter in the first house, and both planets are dominant in the horoscope. Venus is also trine Neptune.

Example 4: Walter Niemann, composer, October 10, 1876, 3:40 p.m., Hamburg

Venus is conjunct Uranus, trine Neptune, and in aspect to the dominant Saturn in the first house. Musicality is very clearly shown, the more so by the conjunction of the Sun and Mercury in Libra, which is in turn trine the Ascendant and sextile the Midheaven—a very striking musical horoscope.

Example 5: Composer, April 30, 1903, 5:00 a.m., Berlin

10th 19 ♑	☉ 8 ♉ 30	♃ 15 ♓
11th 10 ♒	☽ 13 ♊	♂ 28 ♍
12th 14 ♓	♆ 2 ♋	♀ 14 ♊ 30
1st 15 ♉	♅ 25 ♐	☿ 26 ♉ 30
2nd 13 ♊	♄ 9 ♒	
3rd 2 ♋		

The Sun and Ascendant are in the musical sign Taurus. Venus is conjunct the Moon and both are in weak opposition to Uranus.

Example 6: First-violinist of a well-known string quartet, June 27, 1893, 5:00 a.m., Leipzig

10th 16 ♓	☉ 5 ♋	♃ 21 ♉
11th 22 ♈	☽ 13 ♐	♂ 28 ♋
12th 10 ♊	♆ 12 ♊	♀ 21 ♋
1st 19 ♋	♅ 7 ♏	☿ 28 ♋
2nd 3 ♌	♄ 6 ♎	
3rd 21 ♌		

Mars, Venus and Mercury are all conjunct and powerful in Cancer in the first house, as well as in aspect to both Jupiter and the Midheaven. Venus is the dominant planet because it is conjunct the Ascendant and forms the *closest* aspect to Jupiter and the Midheaven.

Example 7: Cellist, January 12, 1902, 4:56 p.m., 53N30, 11E30

10th 1 ♈	☉ 21 ♑ 30	♃ 24 ♑
11th 11 ♉	☽ 24 ♒	♂ 8 ♒
12th 26 ♊	♆ 29 ♊ 30	♀ 0 ♓
1st 29 ♋	♅ 19 ♐	☿ 28 ♑
2nd 14 ♌	♄ 19 ♑	
3rd 8 ♍		

The musical sign Cancer rises, and Venus is in the eighth house trine Neptune and conjunct the Moon.

Example 8: First-violinist, July 11, 1914, 7:00 p.m., 51N, 10E15

The Ascendant in the musical sign Sagittarius receives an exact trine from Venus, which in turn is sextile Saturn, the strongest planet in the horoscope. As is often the case, Mercury is in Cancer.

Example 9: Musician and composer, November 10, 1896, 10:00 a.m., 50N, 8E

10th 15 ♎	☉ 18 ♏ 30	♃ 7 ♍
11th 10 ♏	☽ 26 ♑ ♊♑	♂ 29 ♊
12th 29 ♏	♆ 20 ♊	♀ 20 ♐ 30
1st 16 ♐	♅ 24 ♏ 30	☿ 8 ♏
2nd 24 ♑	♄ 21 ♏ 30	
3rd 9 ♓		

The Ascendant in the musical sign Sagittarius is closely conjunct the dominant Venus, which forms an exact opposition to Neptune.

Example 10: Pianist, September 20, 1902

10th 29 ♍	☉ 27 ♍	♃ 8 ♒
11th 27 ♎	☽ 2 ♉	♂ 10 ♌
12th 19 ♏	♆ 3 ♋ 30	♀ 9 ♍
1st 7 ♐	♅ 19 ♐	☿ 22 ♎ 10
2nd 11 ♑	♄ 21 ♑	
3rd 21 ♒		

The Ascendant in the musical sign Sagittarius receives an exact square from Venus, which, as is frequent in the horoscopes of musicians, is square Uranus—the horoscope's strongest planet—as well as sextile Neptune. Venus also receives other aspects.

Example 11: Violinist, December 4, 1896, just before 12 midnight, 52N, 10E30

10th 12 ♊	☉ 13 ♐ 30	♃ 9 ♍ 30
11th 19 ♋	☽ 16 ♐	♂ 22 ♊ 30
12th 21 ♌	♆ 19 ♊	♀ 20 ♑
1st 16 ♍	♅ 26 ♏	☿ 17 ♐
2nd 8 ♎	♄ 24 ♏	

The Ascendant is in the musical sign Virgo and trine to the fifth house Venus, which in turn is sextile Uranus.

The Actor

As with all the arts, acting talent demands a well-placed Venus. Frequently there are aspects between Mars and Venus, or Mars is also strongly placed, but independent of any Venus aspect. The frequently passionate expression of inner feeling that is requisite for this vocation is shown by the strength of Mars in the horoscope. Venus is often in the tenth, first, or fifth house with an aspect to Mars; the square is as effective as the sextile and. trine, and perhaps even more so. It is not difficult to grasp the fact that the expression of emotional intensity would derive greater stimulus from inharmonious aspects than from harmonious ones, and I personally doubt if the greatest actors ever had harmonious personalities. One must experience suffering , passion, and struggle in order to give it expression that is universally valid.

It is possible that a prominence of the sign Libra can replace a weak Venus, but in practice this is only rarely found. Very frequent is some relationship between the signs Leo and Libra. Moreover, in a large amount of data the Sun was most often in Sagittarius, Aquarius, or Pisces.

There seems to be no specific distribution of planets in the houses, although it may be that the fifth house (instinctual drives, emotion) and the first house are emphasized somewhat beyond the normally expected frequency. The eastern half of the horoscope is usually heavily tenanted, indicating the extraverted temperament as well as the drive toward prominence and recognition.

A distinction should be made between a simple talent for mimicry and the ability to give a convincing portrayal of a total personality. A gift for mimicry is characteristic of the signs Gemini and Cancer, but from a gift of mimicry to a great interpretive performance there is a long distance and the prominent Venus and Mars configuration must be found if the latter is to be expected.

Example 1: Female, December 20, 1896, 9:30 a.m., Dresden

10th 23 ♏	☉ 29 ♐	♃ 10 ♍
11th 12 ♐	☽ 1 ♋	♂ 16 ♊ 30
12th 29 ♐	♆ 18 ♊ 30	♀ 9 ♒
1st 18 ♑	♅ 27 ♏	☿ 11 ♑
2nd 14 ♓	♄ 26 ♏	
3rd 27 ♈		

We find here—as is frequent among actors and singers—the middle decanate of Capricorn rising. Venus is strong in the first house in Aquarius and also aspects Mars and Neptune in the fifth. The Sun is in Sagittarius, a position frequently found among actors, and the Moon is in Cancer, adding the gift of mimicry. Uranus and Saturn in the tenth house indicate serious difficulties in the profession related to character and temperament rather than to lack of talent. Talent is clearly shown in this horoscope. This example shows how mistaken it is to draw vocational conclusions solely from the planets in the tenth house without analyzing the remainder of the horoscope for other indications of ability of equal importance.

Example 2: Josef Kainz, January 2, 1858, 7:20 a.m., Wieselburg, Hungary

This great artist (see page 74) has Venus just in *front* of the rising degree, which adds an intellectual dimension to his otherwise rather sensual style. Venus in the artistic sign Sagittarius is sextile to Mars and this typical acting aspect rules the horoscope. Mercury in the first house with unusually strong aspects points up further the intellectual qualities of this artist as well as his great talent for speaking. There is a hint that this talent results from an over-compensation for lack of innate ability, which is suggested by the adverse aspects received by Mercury.

Example 3: Eleanore Duse, October 15, 1859, sunrise, Vigevano, Italy

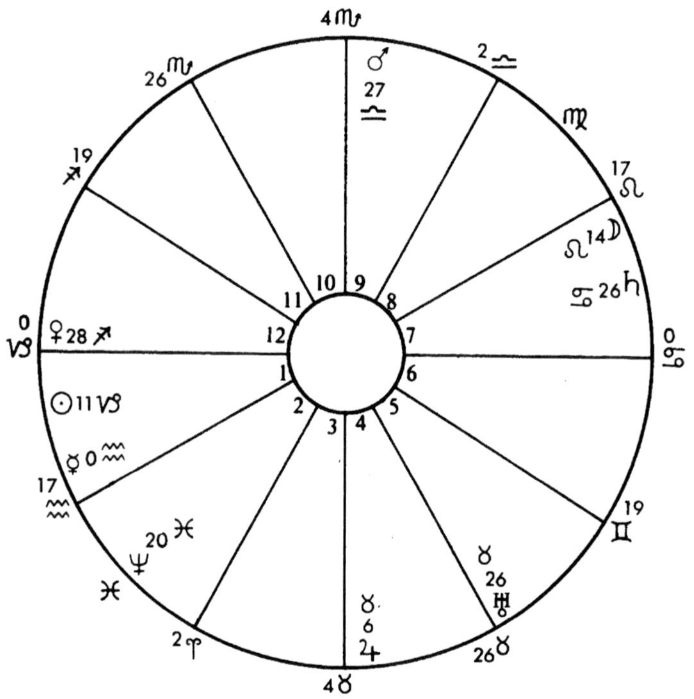

Example 2, Josef Kainz

10th 12 ♋	☉ 11 ♎ 26	♃ 23 ♋
11th 15 ♌	☽ 26 ♑ 28	♂ 16 ♍ 23
12th 15 ♍	♆ 25 ♓ 20	♀ 13 ♎ 20
1st 10 ♎	♅ 7 ♊ 30	☿ 7 ♎
2nd 7 ♏	♄ 20 ♌ 40	
3rd 8 ♐		

Libra, the sign of the stage, rises with the Sun conjunct Venus and Mercury therein, showing at once the fundamental artistic temperament of this great actress. Jupiter in Cancer in the tenth lends intuitive power and symbolizes the actress' great popularity and success. Although the Libra planets by themselves ensure considerable talent for the stage, Mars is nonetheless strong by its sextile to Jupiter in the tenth, and especially by its sextile to the Midheaven.

A clear distinction between talent for the stage and for the screen cannot be made, and the fact that so many stage actors have become screen actors is an indication that there is no essential difference. It has been said that Uranus is more prominent in the horoscopes of screen stars, but this is an unreliable index even though occasionally it may be true.

Example 4: Film actress, December 7, 1896, 6:30 a.m., Berlin

10th 21 ♍	☉ 15 ♐ 30	♃ 9 ♍ 45
11th 21 ♎	☽ 19 ♑	♂ 21 ♊ 33
12th 12 ♏	♆ 19 ♊	♀ 23 ♑
1st 27 ♏	♅ 26 ♏	☿ 20 ♐ 30
2nd 0 ♑	♄ 24 ♏ 30	
3rd 12 ♒		

This actress has the Sun conjunct Mercury in Sagittarius in the first house, which points to the possibility of an acting career. Venus is conjunct the Moon in the second house and has good aspects to the Ascendant and the Midheaven. Uranus is conjunct Saturn on the first house cusp.

The kind of drama in which the actor or actress will appear, or in which he will be most suitable, cannot be determined too clearly by astrology. But one might assume that the actor with many critical aspects, indicating inner disharmony and even depression, would gravitate toward tragedy. Humor and cheerfulness are associated with Taurus in that the typical comedian—fat, round, with short arms and short neck—is distinctly Taurean, but it would be a mistake to assume that such humor results from good aspects. On the contrary, it is usually the result of inner disharmony and difficulties for which the individual tries to provide compensation. Adverse aspects between Mars and Venus, and Mars and Mercury, give a sharp wit, while irony and satire are more Saturnian in nature. The more elegant or grand the actor's style is, the more elements of Leo, Libra, and Sagittarius (or perhaps a combination of all three) will be found.

The Singer

The determination of singing talent by astrology is not completely possible at present. A study of several individual horoscopes has been revealing, but it is not clear to what extent the indications are generally valid. Astrological tradition does speak of "vocal" and "voiceless" signs but my experience shows these distinctions to be worthless. More valid may be the correlation of singing with the sign Taurus, which has always been associated with the throat and larynx. I find that it indicates tenors among men, and sopranos among women, that are clearly influenced by Taurus, but this is not a hard and fast rule. Taurus rising or in the first house seems to enhance singing talent. In the horoscopes of singers the Moon, Mercury, or Venus is frequently found in Taurus, and Venus there almost always indicates the soprano or tenor. The tradition that Mercury or Venus retrograde confers singing talent is also not clearly substantiated, though there may be justification for the assumption that Mercury retrograde may do so. Of course, Venus must be prominent.

Example 1: Singer, March 21, 1900, 1:15 p.m., 51N20, 0E49

10th 16 ♈	☉ 0 ♈ 27	♃ 10 ♐ 48
11th 25 ♉	☽ 28 ♏ 10	♂ 16 ♓ 12
12th 6 ♋	♆ 24 ♊ 17	♀ 12 ♉ 25
1st 7 ♌	♅ 12 ♐ 28	☿ 6 ♈ 56R
2nd 24 ♌	& 4 ♑ 34	
3rd 16 ♍		

Venus in Taurus in the tenth house is the dominant planet, and its sextile to Mars facilitates emotional expression. This is the horoscope of an opera singer and a soprano. In conformity with astrological tradition, Mercury is retrograde, and its strong aspects to the planets in the fifth house increase artistic ability.

Example 2: Singer, March 23, 1900, 6:45 a.m., 51N, 0E55

10th 9 ♑	☉ 2 ♈	♃ 11 ♐
11th 29 ♑	☽ 20 ♐	♂ 17 ♓ 30
12th 27 ♒	♆ 24 ♊	♀ 14 ♉ 30
1st 23 ♈	♅ 12 ♐ 30	☿ 5 ♈ 30R
2nd 0 ♊	♄ 4 ♑ 30	
3rd 21 ♊		

This is the horoscope of a soprano, and Venus in Taurus in the first house is the dominant planet. Aspects are similar to the ones mentioned in the previous example as the two births were only about forty hours apart.

Example 3: World-famous soprano, November 11, 1883, 9:00 a.m., 51N, 0E50

The Ascendant is conjunct Venus and trine Mars. Both these planets are powerful and facilitate emotional expression, but there is no aspect between the two planets if strict orbs are observed. The strong and fortunate Venus indicates this woman's unusual artistic ability.

The Dancer (including gymnastics)

A predominance of the air signs seems to be a requisite for physical agility, and a strong Venus for the esthetic sensibility necessary for dancing. A prominent Sagittarius is particularly helpful as this sign is related to dance, sports, and physical movement in general. Even those Sagittarians who have put on weight or are in poor physical condition nevertheless take great pleasure in dancing and sports. Venus is usually quite strong in the dancer's horoscope, and occasionally it appears in the fifth or eleventh house.

Esthetics often play a part in gymnastics, but a strong Mars indicating muscular strength is also found in most cases. A prominence of Scorpio and the fifth house indicates the interest in teaching that is frequently observed in connection with this vocation.

Example 1: Dancer and instructor in gymnastics, February 14, 1905, 11:45 a.m., 51N20, 0E49

10th 15 ♒	☉ 25 ♒ 06	♃ 25 ♈ 58
11th 13 ♓	☽ 15 ♊ 35	♂ 14 ♏ 21
12th 29 ♈	♆ 5 ♋ 38	♀ 11 ♈ 48
1st 21 ♊	♅ 3 ♑ 03	☿ 7 ♒ 53
2nd 9 ♋	♄ 23 ♒ 40	
3rd 25 ♋		

The Ascendant, Sun, and Moon are in air signs. Venus in Aries is in the eleventh house in aspect with Mercury, Moon, and Uranus (the latter aspect shows musicality).

Example 2: Teacher of eurhythmics and gymnastics, August 3, 1907, 10:00 a.m., 51N20N, 0E49

10th 7 ♋	☉ 9 ♌ 52	♃ 26 ♋ 39
11th 13 ♌	☽ 5 ♊ 23	♂ 7 ♑ 12R
12th 12 ♍	♆ 13 ♋ 25	♀ 28 ♋ 13
1st 5 ♎	♅ 9 ♑ 34R	☿ 26 ♋ 29
2nd 0 ♏	♄ 26 ♓ 58R	
3rd 1 ♐		

The Moon and the Ascendant are in air signs and in an exact trine, while Venus is well placed in the tenth house in conjunction with Mercury and Jupiter. Note that the Leo-Libra combination is found here through the signs occupied by the Sun and the Ascendant. Mars on the cusp of the fourth house provides the necessary physical energy.

Example 3: Teacher of gymnastics, July 17, 1906, noon, 51N20, 0E49

10th 20 ♋	☉ 23 ♋ 56	♃ 27 ♊ 09
11th 25 ♌	☽ 8 ♊ 13	♂ 23 ♋ 26
12th 24 ♍	♆ 10 ♋ 40	♀ 1 ♍ 39
1st 15 ♎	♅ 5 ♑ 47R	☿ 20 ♌ 25
2nd 11 ♏	♄ 14 ♓ 40R	
3rd 12 ♐		

The Ascendant is in the air sign Libra and, as is frequent, the Moon is in Gemini. Venus in the eleventh house is trine Uranus (musicality, rhythm). Mars on the cusp of the tenth house and conjunct the Sun, giving great energy. This woman has an interest in medicine, which is shown by this position of Mars.

Example 4: Teacher of gymnastics, June 9, 1905, 8:45 p.m., 52N30, 1E05

10th 29 ♎	☉ 18 ♊	♃ 22 ♉
11th 21 ♏	☽ 8 ♍ 55	♂ 9 ♏
12th 8 ♐	♆ 7 ♋	♀ 6 ♉
1st 24 ♐	♅ 3 ♑	☿ 2 ♊
2nd 8 ♒	♄ 3 ♓	
3rd 26 ♓		

The Ascendant is in the athletic sign Sagittarius, and energy is provided by the tenth house Mars, while Venus in the fourth house in Taurus gives artistic ability. Venus' aspects with Uranus and Neptune confer musicality and rhythm, and its aspect with Mars indicates the constructive expression of emotion.

Example 5: Teacher of gymnastics, August 20, 1893, 12:30 p.m., 48N, 1E05

10th 6 ♍	☉ 27 ♌ 37	♃ 29 ♉ 58

11th 7 ♎	☽ 9 ♐ 15	♂ 2 ♍ 32
12th 1 ♏	♆ 13 ♊ 22	♀ 26 ♍ 57
1st 20 ♏	♅ 7 ♏ 12	☿ 11 ♌ 18
2nd 20 ♐	♄ 10 ♎ 07	
3rd 27 ♑		

Mars and Venus in the tenth house are the strongest planets in the horoscope and denote artistic ability and the facility of emotional expression. The interest in gymnastics is shown by the Moon in Sagittarius in aspect to Mercury, Mars, Saturn, and Neptune. This Mars position is indicative of this woman's long study of medicine which she utilizes in her profession (gymnastics used for physical therapy). The general scientific interests are shown by the strong Mercury in the ninth house. This woman also studied singing for some time and utilizes this too in her professional work, which incorporates the new ideas of the Sievers-Rutz school.

The Social Professions

The professions that deal directly with the structured order of society are so varied that they cannot be summed up easily, as abilities which relate to other more specific vocations will be found as well in the horoscope. Nevertheless, a concern on the part of the individual for what he construes to be the welfare of society can be seen in the horoscope by a powerful and appropriately placed Jupiter.

The Administrator

The individual who is capable of holding an important administrative position should have in his horoscope a strong Sun and Jupiter, which will enable him to comprehend details but at the same time see the overall view as well as exercise authoritative control (the Sun). A well-placed Saturn is valuable as it imparts the required calmness, patience, and perseverance. Finally, one must look for other abilities in the horoscope to interpret the specific area where administrative capacity is most likely to be exercised.

Administrative capacity in any area of finance will be seen by planets in the second house. Where conscientious application to details is required, there should be an emphasis on Virgo, or a strong but not too extraverted Mercury, receiving favorable aspects from Saturn.

The capacity to represent the interests of others—in politics as well as elsewhere—is seen by a strong Sun or a predominance of the sign Leo. Where it is desirable that these qualities be found in combination with a certain adroitness and tact, a Libra emphasis is found.

In the vocational areas described above, adverse aspects are undesirable as everything here depends on the ability to work with and get along with other persons and groups, and the insistence on one's own points of view, which is commonly found where there are adverse aspects, makes work within an organization difficult. Also undesirable are the unfavorable aspects of Jupiter to Neptune as these indicate a susceptibility to outside influence that can seduce one from the straight and narrow path. Those times when Jupiter or Neptune transit the natal aspect will prove to be the most dangerous.

The Lawyer

Not all lawyers are in the service of the public welfare, and of only very few could this be said at all. In most instances the lawyer is an individual whose wits assist in his client's conflict with society, and for this reason we find Mercury stronger than Jupiter in the horoscope. The influence of Mercury can be further amplified by an emphasis on the signs Gemini and Virgo. The sign typical of the defense counsel who knows how to argue with conviction from any point of view is Gemini, which to some extent always confers a talent for conversation and debate. Virgo is better at the behind-the-scenes preparation of cases involving intricate legal problems.

Example 1: Attorney, May 12, 1897, 5:00 a.m., 51N20, 0E50

10th 1 ♒	☉ 21 ♉ 39	♃ 0 ♍ 36
11th 25 ♒	☽ 20 ♍ 11	♂ 26 ♋ 26
12th 6 ♈	♆ 18 ♊ 56	♀ 1 ♉ 49
1st 4 ♊	♅ 27 ♏ 17	☿ 4 ♊ 24R
2nd 25 ♊	♄ 27 ♏ 56	
3rd 12 ♋		

The Ascendant in Gemini indicates rapid assimilation of the most diverse points of view as well as fluency of speech and a gift for debate. Mercury in the first house is the dominant planet and helps augment the Gemini influence, while its opposition to Saturn and Uranus suggest that the fluency of speech has been accomplished through the overcoming of some innate difficulty or inhibition. The Sun and Moon in earth signs give objectivity and a realistic point of view. The inner disharmonies shown by the unfavorable aspects in this horoscope may grant an insight into those problems of human life that so frequently end up in the courts.

The judge must naturally have a stronger Jupiter, which corresponds to an increased sense of social responsibility. Authority is shown by a strong Sun, or an emphasis on the sign Leo. There is a distinct parallel with teaching, except that the feeling for the abnormal and the anti-social is absent in the latter profession.

The best lawyer is probably one who in resolving his own inner conflicts with society finally opts for the support of traditional social values, and for this reason planets are found in the twelfth house in almost all lawyers' horoscopes. In contrast with the horoscopes of physicians, however, different signs will be stressed, and there will be no planets in the sixth house. Mars is never found to be as prominent as in the horoscopes of physicians, although aspects between Mars and the Sun, or occasionally Mars and the Moon, occur frequently in the horoscopes of lawyers who hanker after power and recognition.

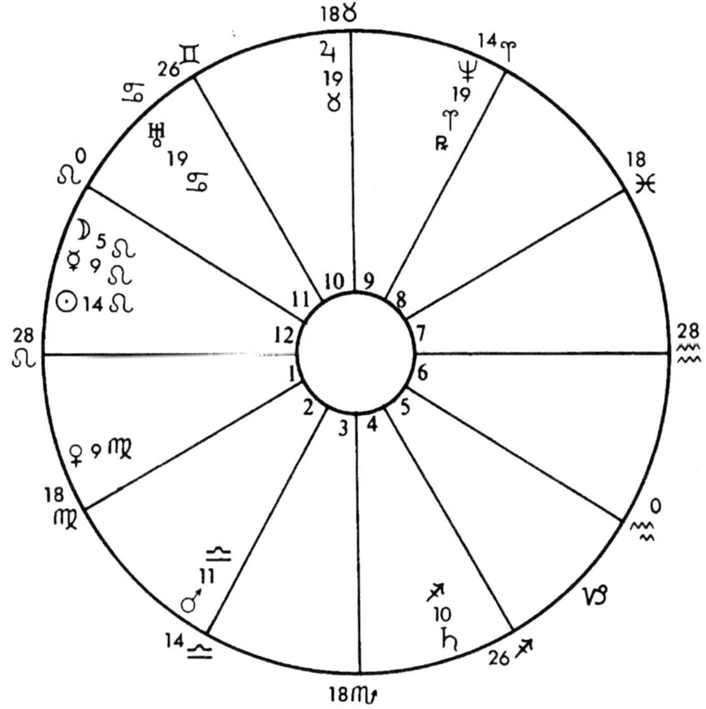

Example 2, Director of a County Court

Example 2: Director of a county court, August 7, 1869, 6:00 a.m., 50N30, 12E30

The Ascendant, Sun, Moon and Mercury are in the authoritative sign of Leo, and the Sun and Moon are in the twelfth house, indicating the subjective connection with social abnormality. Mars is sextile both the Sun and Moon, showing energy as well as the field to which it is directed. The horoscope is ruled by Jupiter in the tenth house—the planet that best represents the will of society.

The Politician

Again there is difficulty describing clearly and briefly the specific indications of ability in politics because an interest in this field can be based on quite varied motives.

The statesman whose main interest is foreign policy will have planets in the ninth house, showing the desire to control or manipulate events at the widest possible level. Such a statesman, who is successful through his use of caution, adaptability, diplomacy, and understanding of hard facts will have planets in the earth signs in the ninth house or elsewhere in the horoscope. Subtlety and diplomatic finesse are frequently seen by aspects of Mercury to Neptune. The politician who is motivated by a desire for power through revolution and drastic change will show a predominance of the fire signs in the ninth house or elsewhere.

Example 1: Gustav Stresemann, May 10, 1878, 12:30 p.m., Berlin

10th 28 ♉	☉ 19 ♉ 38	♃ 6 ♒ 48
11th 6 ♋	☽ 26 ♌ 43	♂ 2 ♋ 40
12th 10 ♌	♆ 7 ♉ 43	♀ 3 ♈ 46
1st 6 ♍	♅ 25 ♌ 21	☿ 13 ♉ 50
2nd 27 ♍	♄ 29 ♓ 36	
3rd 24 ♎		

The planets in the ninth house give an inclination for foreign affairs, and the prominence of earth signs shows practicality and a knack for getting things done. The conjunction of Mercury and Neptune in Taurus in the ninth house is a brilliant indication of diplomatic subtlety and finesse. The many adverse aspects in the horoscope show that popularity has been difficult to attain.

Example 2: Bismarck, April 1, 1815, 1:08 p.m., Schonhausen

10th 4 ♉	☉ 11 ♈	♃ 4 ♎ 30
11th 14 ♊	☽ 9 ♑	♂ 1 ♒

12th 21 ♋	♆ 20 ♐	♀ 4 ♉
1st 19 ♌	♅ 7 ♐	☿ 17 ♓
2nd 8 ♍	♄ 10 ♒	
3rd 2 ♎		

Fire signs on the Ascendent and in the ninth house coupled with the Sun in Aries provide an outstanding example of the power politician.

Example 3: Benito Mussolini, July 29, 1883, 2:00 p.m., Varano, Italy.

10th 4 ♍	☉ 6 ♌	♃ 18 ♋ 30
11th 6 ♎	☽ 9 ♊	♂ 13 ♊
12th 1 ♏	♆ 21 ♉	♀ 21 ♋ 30
1st 22 ♏	♅ 21 ♍	☿ 5 ♌ 30
2nd 24 ♐	♄ 7 ♊ 30	
3rd 28 ♑		

The mixture of fire and earth signs describes a power politician with a strong sense of practical realities. A taste for the financial aspect of politics can be seen by planets in the second house.

Example 4: Male, February 20,1898, 3:45 a.m., 51N, 0E50

10th 26 ♎	☉ 1 ♓ 30	♃ 9 ♎
11th 19 ♏	☽ 22 ♒	♂ 7 ♒ 30
12th 7 ♐	♆ 20 ♊	♀ 2 ♓ 30
1st 22 ♐	♅ 3 ♐ 30	☿ 13 ♒
2nd 5 ♒	♄ 11 ♐ 30	
3rd 22 ♓		

The Moon, Mercury, Mars, Sun, and Venus are in the second house, indicating a talent for finance. Mercury in Aquarius and conjunct both the Moon and Mars describe an unusually active and disputatious intellect. The administrative politician should show a strong Sun and Jupiter in the horoscope as these indicate authority and organizational ability.

Example 1: Friedrich Ebert, February 4, 1871, noon, Heidelberg

10th 12 ♒	☉ 15 ♒ 17	♃ 16 ♊ 27
11th 10 ♓	☽ 2 ♌ 20	♂ 8 ♎ 02
12th 24 ♈	♆ 19 ♈ 25	♀ 29 ♒ 09
1st 16 ♊	♅ 23 ♋ 43	☿ 20 ♑ 30
2nd 5 ♋	♄ 5 ♑ 49	
3rd 22 ♋		

The trine of the Sun to Jupiter rules the horoscope and indicates a talent for organization. For decades, this man served his party and only gradually reached the highest possible position president of the new German republic. Mercury in the earth sign Capricorn in the ninth house is an indication of Ebert's desire to handle in an objective way the most diverse problems of foreign policy, which were quite beyond the sphere of national or administrative politics.

In general, one frequently finds the sign Capricorn prominent among politicians. Those born under this sign are well known for their ambition and the perseverance they show in pursuit of their goals. Libra, on the other hand, describes the politician who courts the favor of the masses and secures his political influence by close personal contact with the public. The champion of the working classes will have planets in the sixth house. Personality traits conducive to popularity are shown by aspects of the Moon to Jupiter, but favorable aspects between the Sun and Moon also show success through popularity. When a good aspect between the Moon and Jupiter rules the horoscope, continuous success in politics is assured. If such an aspect is weaker by position in the horoscope, popularity may well be attained, but other configurations can rob the aspect of its continuing power.

Example 2: Adolf Hitler, April 20, 1889, 6:30 p.m., Braunau

10th 4 ♌	☉ 0 ♉ 50	♃ ♏ 0
11th 8 ♍	☽ 7 ♑	♂ 16 ♉ 30
12th 5 ♎	♆ 1 ♊	$ 16 ♉ 45
1st 27 ♎	♅ 19 ♎ 30	☿ 25 ♈ 42
2nd 24 ♏	♄ 13 ♌ 30	
3rd 27 ♐		

Libra on the Ascendant and many planets in the seventh house denote a public figure who maintains his political influence by personal contact with the public. The Moon-Jupiter conjunction in Capricorn in the third house trine the Sun in the seventh points out character traits that sound a note of response in the public at large so that a rapport of popularity is established. Ultimate success is beset by difficulties, however, because of the relatively weak position of the Moon-Jupiter conjunction in the third house, as well as by the position of Saturn in the tenth.

Example 3: Paul von Hindenburg, October 2, 1847, 3:00 p.m., Posen

10th 28 ♏	☉ 8 ♎ 45	♃ 18 ♋ 30
11th 16 ♐	☽ 23 ♋ 30	♂ 15 ♉
12th 3 ♑	♆ 28 ♒	♀ 10 ♎ 30
1st 23 ♑	♅ 16 ♈ 30	☿ 18 ♎
2nd 22 ♓	♄ 7 ♓ 30	
3rd 3 ♉		

The conjunction of the Moon and Jupiter in Cancer in the seventh house rules the horoscope and gives some indication of the outstanding humane qualities that have won the affection and respect of the entire nation. Of all the rather difficult aspects in this horoscope, the one that is the most favorable for popularity and success is dominant so that despite all the blows of fate, the trust of the majority of the people has not been shaken. The Ascendant in Capricorn confers that energy and persistence, as well as ambition, that enabled Hindenburg to rise to the rank of a commanding general long before he began a political career. It must be said, though, that this horoscope is not one of an outstanding strategist but much more of the man of unquestionable principle and humaneness. The Sun, Mercury, and Venus in Libra give impartial judgment and the capacity to settle arguments. The strong Jupiter shows the ability to serve with success the general welfare of society.

The Soldier and the Police Officer

A military career at a higher level is not to be thought of simply as a Mars vocation. Courage, combativeness, and love of power (Mars-Sun) are fundamental character traits for this group, but they must be found together with the ability to comprehend and evaluate complex military problems. This ability is reflected by Mars-Mercury aspects, which are found in the horoscopes of outstanding strategists (Frederick the Great, Ludendorff, Hotzendorf, Foch). Pedagogical abilities also fall within the range of these aspects and also seem to be present in most cases. Some prominence of the signs Aries or Scorpio is not unusual (Ludendorff, Hotzendorf) and Leo is even more frequently found to be of importance in the horoscope. As a military career is hardly possible in the Germany of today, only brief notes are given for this group.

Example 1: General Erich Ludendorff. The Ascendant is in Leo, while the Sun in Aries is dominant. Mars in the twelfth house has several aspects, including an exact square to the Midheaven and a sextile to Mercury in the tenth house. This is an outstanding military horoscope. Aries, Leo, Mars, and the Sun reflect combativeness and love of power, and the Mercury-Mars aspect indicates talent for military science as well as for instruction.

Example 2: Conrad von Hotzendorf. The Sun and Moon are in Scorpio in the tenth house. Mars is conjunct Mercury in the eleventh house.

Example 3: Marshall Foch. Mercury in Virgo is the dominant planet and is sextile Mars near the end of the first house, indicating pedagogical talent and interest in military science. However, with the Sun in Libra, and Cancer rising, there is little aggressiveness or love of battle.

At the lower levels of military organization, as well as among the civilian police, a strong Mars is essential and is usually the dominant planet in these horoscopes, more frequently by placement in an angular house than by aspect to an angular cusp. This indicates action and performance rather than the consideration of theoretical problems.

Example 4: Police sergeant, April 15, 1888, 10:00 a.m., 53N, 13E55

10th 24 ♓	☉ 25 ♈ 50	♃ 5 ♐ 28
11th 1 ♉	☽ 9 ♊ 47	♂ 20 ♎ 14
12th 17 ♊	♆ 28 ♉ 30	♀ 2 ♈ 40
1st 24 ♋	♅ 14 ♎ 46	☿ 2 ♈ 30
2nd 9 ♌	♄ 29 ♋ 49	
3rd 28 ♌		

Aries is prominent, and Mars is strong in the fourth house. This man became involved in irregularities and ended up in jail (Jupiter square Neptune).

Example 5: Police commissar, November 5, 1881, 7:30 p.m., 52N, 0E44

10th 6 ♓	☉ 13 ♏ 31	♃ 22 ♉
11th 10 ♈	☽ 9 ♉ 43	♂ 14 ♋ 30
12th 28 ♉	♆ 15 ♉	♀ 18 ♎
1st 10 ♋	♅ 17 ♍ 30	☿ 19 ♏
2nd 25 ♋	♄ 8 ♉ 36	
3rd 13 ♌		

The sign Scorpio is prominent, and Mars in the first house is the dominant planet. This man was also involved in irregularities and went to jail (Jupiter conjunct Neptune).

Example 6: Police sergeant, June 2, 1879, 6:30 p.m., Wilkau

10th 17 ♍	☉ 12 ♊	♃ 11 ♓ 30
11th 17 ♎	☽ 16 ♏	♂ 25 ♓ 30
12th 8 ♏	♆ 11 ♉	♀ 22 ♋ 30
1st 25 ♏	♅ 0 ♍ 30	☿ 24 ♉
2nd 27 ♐	♄ 13 ♈ 30	
3rd 8 ♒		

Scorpio is once again prominent, and Mars in the first house is the dominant planet.

Example 7: Police sergeant, December 10, 1878, 5:00 a.m., 50N20, 11E

10th 2 ♍	☉ 18 ♐	♃ 6 ♒
11th 4 ♎	☽ 22 ♊	♂ 20 8
12th 27 ♎	♆ 7 ♉ 30	♀ 19 ♐
1st 16 ♏	♅ 4 ♍	☿ 8 ♑ 30
2nd 15 ♐	♄ 26 ♓	
3rd 23 ♑		

Scorpio is strong and Mars is in the first house and dominant.

The horoscopes of these lower military or police echelons can be distinguished from those of physicians, and particularly from surgeons, by the fact that Mercury is usually much weaker, and there are no planets in the sixth or twelfth houses. Locksmiths and blacksmiths have Mars-Jupiter and Mars-Uranus aspects (or the prominence of both planets through position in angular houses or aspects to angular cusps), but these aspects to Mars do not occur in the horoscopes now under consideration. On the other hand,

Mars-Sun aspects are quite frequent. Theoretically at least, there should be some difficulty distinguishing between these horoscopes and those of sculptors, but in practice errors can be avoided by considering all other elements of the horoscope that can give some inkling of the individual's general personality, and of course, if there is prior knowledge of the environment, no mistakes are likely to be made.

Business

There are several kinds of people with business acumen. For example, one acquires fortune and property through large-scale, perhaps somewhat risky, business ventures, while another sets aside what he can and accumulates his capital penny by penny. The latter is more firmly established and remains active within a limited sphere, while the former tries to extend his business into other areas as well. Finally, many seem to be in business without having any special aptitude for it.

Commerce and business are a function of the planet Mercury, which is quite different from the Mercury of the scholar, and in the horoscope of the business person a strong Mercury is always desirable; its placement in an angular house, particularly in the first or tenth, is best. In this context Mercury is most advantageous in the earth and water signs Taurus, Cancer, Virgo, Scorpio, Capricorn, and Pisces, although these sign positions are of secondary importance and should not be overestimated.

The position of Mercury is not the only important consideration in the business person's horoscope, however, and its influence can be supplemented by other configurations or even replaced by them. The ability to foresee possibilities of expansion or improvement and to plan accordingly is frequently indicated by aspects between Mercury and Jupiter or by both planets being strongly placed in the horoscope. The adverse aspects do not appear nearly as harmful as might be supposed.

The amassing of capital is quite frequently observed when there are important planets in the second house. Where this second house emphasis is lacking it is almost always an indication that profits through exchange are favored more than the accumulation and preservation of acquired or inherited wealth. Holding onto money is very difficult when the Sun and Mars are in the second house. The ability to obtain money is indicated by these positions, but there will be a lack of thriftiness or wise distribution of funds, and extravagant living depletes the resources, or income is too rapidly invested in new business ventures. If Mars or the Sun in this house receive bad aspects, there is always a serious threat to one's resources. The aspects of Saturn to these planets—and particularly to the Sun—have an opposite effect. These denote thriftiness, careful handling of money, and occasionally, avarice. If these aspects are adverse, they create deep-seated anxieties and conflicts over money and possessions that bring a whole train of problems in their wake.

Saturn in the second house (under favorable aspect) describes a person of thrift, economy, and caution who works steadily and accumulates wealth by putting capital into sound investments or real estate. The same is true of most aspects between planets in the second and fourth houses. In fact, a favorable Saturn strongly placed anywhere in the horoscope will result in the careful investment or handling of money, but if in the second house, the tendency is all the more pronounced. An adverse second house Saturn leads to losses and even deprivation through very poor judgment and sometimes over exaggerated caution. Remember that the desire to acquire money and possessions and to accumulate resources is at all times shown by a powerful Saturn (although these traits need not necessarily be a part of the business person's personality). In such cases, stability—the true gift of Saturn—is characteristic, and the favorable aspects of Saturn with the Sun or Moon confer the required stability of character, tenacity, and perseverance.

On the other hand, a strong Mars in the horoscope, as well as the prominence of the fire signs, indicates an enterprising spirit, courage, and daring, and the energy to see things through to the end, and frequently a talent for publicity when Mars is in aspect to Uranus.

Those business people who calculate their long-range interests with precision and care have earth signs prominent. The sign Virgo in particular represents carefulness in the observation of detail, which explains this sign's affinity with bookkeeping, accounting and calculation, while Gemini, or any of the air and fire signs, show the tendency toward extensive and diverse ramifications in business. Planets in the ninth house show foreign contacts or business on a wide geographical scale, while planets in the fifth house are favorable for speculation as well as predicting trends; they also frequently indicate one who deals in foodstuffs. Speculation is assisted by the good aspects of Jupiter to Uranus as these confer the knack for spotting movements and trends.

The independent business person will have planets in the angular houses, as well as a strong Sun and Jupiter, which show authority and organizational ability.

The business employee par excellence will not have the marked angular house positions as will the self-employed person. Virgo prominent in the horoscope, or Mercury-Saturn aspects—preferably in earth signs—are all helpful for bookkeeping and accounting where carefulness and exactness are required. On the other hand, the really good secretary should have Gemini or the air signs prominent as these comprehend rapidly and work with greater speed. The business person who travels extensively should speak well, be energetic and active, and be able to convince others. The earth signs are not conducive to these personality traits; a strong Mercury, however, in aspect to either the Moon or Mars, is ideal in the horoscope of such a person.

It is not feasible to describe all the possibilities that might be of importance in the area of business, but if the horoscope is evaluated with reasonable accuracy in terms of general character traits and abilities, it should not be too difficult to decide what the most suitable kind of business profession would be.

Example 1: Business person, publisher, advertiser, December 22, 1889, 9:00 a.m., 53N, 0E42

10th 19 ♏	☉ 0 ♑ 45	♃ 15 ♑ 30
11th 8 ♐	☽ 28 ♐	♂ 24 ♎ 30
12th 24 ♐	♆ 2 ♊ 30	♀ 17 ♐
1st 10 ♑	♅ 26 ♎	☿ 9 ♑
2nd 6 ♓	♄ 4 ♍	
3rd 22 ♈		

Capricorn, the sign of ambition and business acumen, rises. Mercury conjunct Jupiter on the Ascendant rules the horoscope and confers vision and perspective in practical affairs, as well as constructive ambition. The Ascendant, Sun, Mercury, and Jupiter in Capricorn indicate unusual ambition and perseverance, while the trine of Saturn to the Sun, Moon, and Mercury increases the traits of steadiness and perseverance, and indicates acquisitiveness and love of possessions. Since the horoscope does not show any planets in the second house, money will come in the form of the usual business profits. Although it will not be carelessly distributed, neither will it lead to the amassing of capital, but rather profits will be invested in the expansion of the business itself, its merchandise, and so forth (Saturn trine the Sun, Moon and Mercury).

Mars and Uranus in close conjunction in the ninth house show the interests in publishing as well as technology. They also reveal his talent for publicity work, and the desire to propagandize his own ideas and opinions.

Example 2: Hugo Stinnes, February 12, 1870, 8:00 a.m., Muhlheim

10th 22 ♐	☉ 23 ♒ 30	♃ 13 ♉ 30
11th 11 ♑	☽ 4 ♋	♂ 29 ♒ 30

12th 2 ♒	♆ 17 ♈	♀ 11 ♓
1st 11 ♓	♅ 19 ♋	☿ 6 ♒
2nd 5 ♉	♄ 26 ♐	
3rd 3 ♊		

As in example one, there is an emphasis on the twelfth house, which among business people frequently indicates a behind-the-scenes role and a withdrawal from a purely personal and direct handling of affairs. Jupiter is well placed in the second house and has favorable aspects; the strongest is the sextile to the Ascendant and the dominant Venus there, which indicates vision and resourcefulness in the sphere of economics and finance, as well as steadily increasing and well-managed capital. The aspect to the Moon in the fourth house shows investment in merchandise and real estate, and the very strong Saturn in the tenth house gives stability, acquisitiveness, and love of possessions. The sextile of Jupiter to the fifth house Uranus shows clearly the talent for speculation and sensing future trends.

Example 3: Male, August 21, 1880, 3:00 a.m., 49N, 0E48

10th 16 ♈	☉ 28 ♌	♃ 19 ♈
11th 25 ♉	☽ 10 ♓	♂ 19 ♍ 30
12th 4 ♋	♆ 14 ♉	♀ 9 ♍
1st 6 ♌	♅ 9 ♍	☿ 10 ♌
2nd 23 ♌	♄ 10 ♌	
3rd 15 ♍		

In this horoscope there is no true aspect between Mercury and Jupiter as they are too distant from each other. But these planets together rule the horoscope by their respective positions in the first and tenth houses, so that a talent for business is clearly shown. The Sun is in the second house. From modest beginnings, this man became very rich in banking. Setbacks came later. The strong emphasis on the fire signs tended to over extension of goals, and the opposition between the Moon in the eighth house and the conjunction of Venus and Uranus in the second house reveals an inner irritability that eventually worked out in his financial dealings as well. This banker's unusual character promises a recouping of fortunes through personal strength and sheer ability, however.

Trades

With respect to determining from the horoscope a talent for the various trades, as well as the skills related to these trades, it would be wise not to expect too much as a very high percentage of people in these trades have no special talents at all. The minimum amount of skill required in their performance is possessed by any normal man, and those who really excel at their trade are few and do not remain tradesmen for long. Most people take up a trade because it is about the only opportunity that is open to them. For some of these trades an aptitude will be shown in the horoscope, while for others there appear to be no indications whatsoever. For example, despite the fact that I happen to have considerable data on masons, I have been unable to find any common denominator that would seem to relate to this trade from a consideration of all the horoscopes.

Many of these trades require considerable physical strength, and this is seen by an emphasis on the fire signs as well as a strong Mars in the horoscope. Others require manual dexterity, which is more related to the air signs, while those that demand care and close attention should have the earth signs in greater prominence. The high degree of manual dexterity that is necessary for fine handiwork is best shown by aspects of Mars to Mercury, either favorable or unfavorable. In trades such as locksmiths, mechanics, locomotive engineers, drivers, etc., where mechanical ability is required, Mars and Uranus are almost always strong, either by aspect to one another, or by the relative strength of both in the horoscope.

Locksmiths and mechanics, who must possess both manual dexterity and mechanical ability, have a strong Mars—either in an angular house, in aspect to an angular house cusp, or in aspect to one of the horoscope's strongest planets. Also, Mars-Uranus and Mars-Mercury aspects are common. The Moon seems to be found more frequently in Virgo.

Example 1: Locksmith, June 10, 1905, 3:30 p.m., 51N, 0E53

10th 7 ♌	☉ 19 ♊	♃ 22 ♉
11th 11 ♍	☽ 19 ♍ 30	♂ 8 ♏ 30
12th 8 ♎	♆ 7 ♋	♀ 6 ♉ 30
1st 28 ♎	♅ 3 ♑	☿ 3 ♊ 30
2nd 25 ♏	♄ 3 ♓	
3rd 29 ♐		

Libra, which may indicate mechanical skill, rises, and Mars in the first house is the horoscope's dominant planet. Its sextile to Uranus increases mechanical ability. Mercury is strong because of its sextile to the Midheaven, indicating intelligence and manual dexterity.

Example 2: Locksmith, April 13, 1902, 10:30 p.m., 53N, 0E56.

Sagittarius—sometimes indicating physical strength—rises and Uranus in the first house receives a trine from Mars, indicating mechanical skill. The strong Mercury is a sign of manual dexterity.

In another horoscope of a locksmith which I have at hand the Ascendant is exactly sextile Mars and Uranus, and trine Mercury; in a fourth before me Mars is in the tenth house, sextile Mercury and in opposition to Uranus.

The horoscopes of truck drivers are frequently similar to those of mechanics and usually show a strong Mars. The Mars-Uranus aspects are found, but not so frequently as in the horoscopes of mechanics and locksmiths. Mars-Jupiter aspects seem quite common, giving mechanical ability; they may also indicate an interest in sports and athletics. The Moon is often in Virgo or Scorpio.

Example 1: Truck driver, February 26, 1883, 11:15 p.m., 50N30, 0E49

10th 23 ♌	☉ 8 ♓	♃ 21 3 30
11th 26 ♍	☽ 2 ♏	♂ 18 ♒ 30
12th 20 ♎	♆ 16 ♉	♀ 21 ♑ 30
1st 9 ♏	♅ 22 ♍	☿ 11 ♒ 30
2nd 7 ♐	♄ 20 ♉ 30	
3rd 14 ♑		

The Moon is in Scorpio, and Scorpio rises. Mars conjunct Mercury on the cusp of the fourth house rules the horoscope, and the trine of Mars to Jupiter shows the interest in mechanics as well as in athletics.

Example 2: Truck driver, May 29, 1893, 6:00 a.m., 51N30, 0E52

Mars in the first house is the dominant planet and forms a trine with Uranus and a sextile to Jupiter, indicating mechanical ability; the Moon is in Scorpio. This is the horoscope of a criminal who murdered his victim following a sexual assault (Mars square Saturn, planets in the twelfth house).

In the horoscope of a chauffeur, the Ascendant is trine Mars and the Sun, which are both conjunct in Aries and form the strongest configuration in the horoscope. Mars is sextile Jupiter. Uranus forms an exact aspect to the Moon's North Node near the cusp of the tenth house.

In another such horoscope the Ascendant is sextile Mars, and Mars is trine to Uranus and square Jupiter.

Among the horoscopes of tailors, I find that both Mars and Venus are usually strongly placed, but Mars usually somewhat more so. Aspects between the two planets are very common. Libra, Sagittarius, and Taurus are the signs most frequently rising, or they are emphasized by planets located therein. Aspects of Mars to Jupiter are also frequently found.

My personal experience with horoscopes relating to these trades is limited, and no further conclusions are possible at present. From my own experience, however, I find the tradition that Leo rules those who do fine work in gold to be quite accurate.

SUCCESS AND FAILURE IN THE VOCATION

Not only is it possible to determine from the horoscope the most suitable type of vocation, but also possible to evaluate in a general way the individual's probable success or failure within that vocation. The character and abilities shown in the horoscope offer clues to the outcome that may be expected. Personality problems and character defects such as carelessness, poor judgment, and indiscretion can be learned from the horoscope, as well as positive traits that may assist in achieving a successful career. These undesirable personality traits may result in difficulties during the course of the career, but an understanding of the way these difficulties are rooted in defects of character enables one to grasp more readily the cause of misfortunes which would otherwise seem to be inexplicable. Of course, if the individual is able to correct these defects, an improvement in the course of events is bound to follow. It may not be likely that an accurate interpretation of the horoscope would in itself preclude any further difficulties, but most people would not persist in an unreasonable course of action after gaining some real insight into the cause of their problems.

One of the major obstacles in achieving success in the vocation is the desire to avoid conflict because of feeling insufficiently capable of coping with it. This "no-conflict ideal" can appear along with any of the twelve signs, but its expression in the horoscope will be different depending on the planetary positions and signs involved. The fear of conflict with the environment is somewhat typical of all the negative signs, but in particular of Cancer, Virgo, and Pisces. Persons born under these signs frequently avoid conflict and shun competition because of feelings of inferiority based on some notion of sheer physical inadequacy. Similar attitudes are found with a strongly placed but adverse Saturn, and in particular with the unfavorable aspects of the Moon and Saturn; here the square is worse than the conjunction or opposition. In extreme cases one frequently finds badly aspected planets in the eighth house, which can indicate an addiction to alcohol or drugs. In general, planets strongly placed in the angular houses provide the best protection against the no-conflict ideal, and even adverse aspects to the angular cusps or to planets in the angular houses are rather to be considered as favorable because they result in a tendency to overcompensate for whatever weakness one may recognize. Here again, Saturn and the Moon are an exception, as their conjunction or square can paralyze the urge to act, as described above.

When cardinal and fire signs are pronounced, or when Mars and Uranus are strongly placed, the no-conflict ideal is expressed in a different way. There is a certain fear of confronting one's own inner self, and the struggle with inner insecurities may take the form of conflict with the environment. Thus, one's conflict with the environment may reveal the nature of what is to be overcome within one's self, and a preoccupation with superficial problems may conceal a reluctance to face up to inner inadequacies.

It should not be supposed that adverse aspects always predispose to failure. If the planets involved are strongly placed, they more likely indicate the individual of strong character who must go his own way in the struggle with personal shortcomings. In such cases, life presents many conflicts, and these can frequently be more clearly determined from an analysis of the horoscope. Such inner disequilibrium leads to serious difficulties encountered in life that are not overcome without a long struggle.

Failure is usually indicated in the horoscope when birth occurs at that moment when the general planetary pattern for the day cannot express itself to best advantage through the relationship of important planets to the angular houses. Lack of placements in angular houses and aspects of the planets to the angular cusps is unfavorable for ability and strength of character and predisposes to failure. However, when considering the aspects of planets in the angular houses, it should be noted that the Moon in adverse aspect to Saturn or Uranus (especially the square) is unfavorable for success because of the considerable susceptibility to outside influence shown by this position. An adverse Saturn dominating the horoscope, without mitigating aspects or other factors, is also evil. Further, one should note that the opposition is never as bad as the square. The opposition is an aspect of tension and struggle, while the square is an aspect of paralysis. An excess of critical aspects in the angular houses is unfavorable because the health can be seriously affected, and here the oppositions are no exception, particularly when Uranus, Saturn, or Mars are involved. In the horoscope of Nietzsche, the opposition of Mercury and Mars, as well as of Uranus and Jupiter, are indications of his combative nature; but at the same time these oppositions show illnesses resulting from overexertion and nervous strain. The horoscopes of famous persons frequently contain planets in opposition from angular houses but the opposing planets receive trines and sextiles from other planets, thereby introducing some neutralizing or mitigating effect, as in the horoscopes of Frederick the Great, Goethe, Nietzsche, Ludendorff, and Richard Strauss. Or the opposing planets stand in favorable aspect to the Ascendant and Midheaven, as in the horoscope of Hugo von Hofmannsthal. The so-called bad aspects of Venus and Jupiter need not cause much concern as long as Saturn, Uranus, or Mars are not the aspecting planets and stronger by position. Such aspects show minor difficulties, but have not the power to bring forth anything really serious.

A strong Uranus in the cardinal or mutable signs, and with aspects to the angular cusps or the Sun or Moon, can be a threat to success because the inclinations and opinions of such a person change too frequently, and this is a drawback where strength of purpose is required. In such a case, planets and angular cusps in the fixed signs can provide compensation except for Aquarius, which is of little help because of its excessive impulsiveness.

Decidedly favorable for success is a strong Jupiter, because it provides the imagination and broad outlook that are necessary to make the best of the opportunities and resources available, and because it facilitates cooperation with others. As a rule, an adverse but strong Jupiter is better for success than a favorable but weak one (see the horoscope of Zille and Emperor William II). Naturally, a Jupiter both strong and favorable provides the best prospects (see the horoscope of Friedrich Ebert).

Following are three horoscopes that will illustrate the above points.

Example 1

This horoscope is ruled by the Moon and Uranus, in square and in cardinal signs. This indicates eccentricity (Uranus) in one's manner of living (Moon), and it will have a disastrous affect on the prospects for a successful career because this Uranus-Moon aspect is typical of the Bohemian, who wants to avoid all obligations and commitments. The fact that birth took place when the planetary pattern for that day had reached a relationship to the angles that allowed maximum expression of certain important factors shows that this individual's character and endowments will not be average. The strong favorable aspect between Uranus and the Sun conjunct Mercury indicates no lack of overall ability, and the trine of Uranus to Mercury shows considerable intellectual capacities and originality and inventive talent in some area of technology. The Sun and Mercury in Aquarius and in aspect to Uranus—the strongest planet in the horoscope—shows an interest in psychology and this position and aspect of Mercury indicates some ability in science. However, Mercury's position is not strong enough to overcome the powerful Moon-Uranus square; all intellectual activity

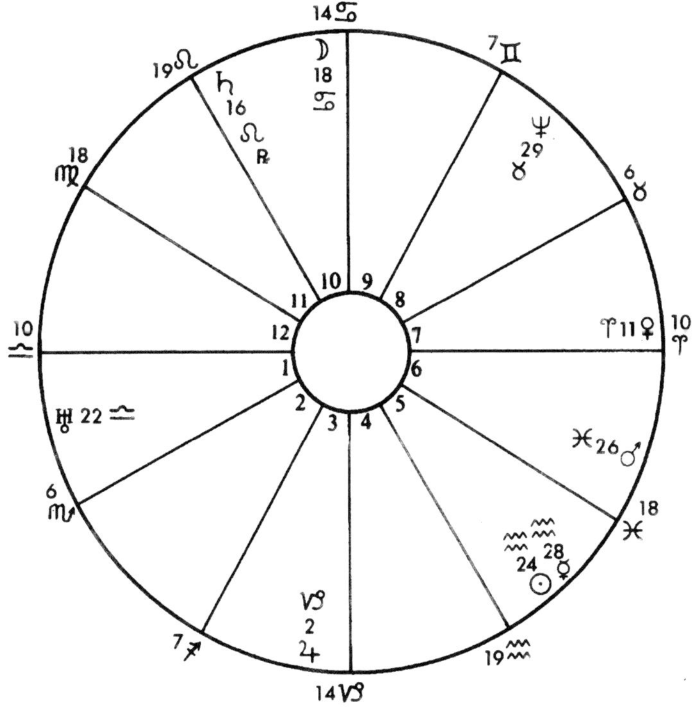

Example 1

must work against the tendencies shown by this aspect. Furthermore, Jupiter and Mars have no essential relationship with the angular cusps or planets in angular houses. Venus on the seventh house cusp shows artistic abilities—probably in the theater—as the Moon is in Cancer (mimicry) and Libra rises. But Venus is also unable to successfully counteract the Moon-Uranus square because on the one hand, the seventh house is weaker than the first and tenth, and on the other, Venus itself is caught up in the Moon-Uranus square through its rather wide square to the Moon. So it will be difficult to find some activity that could encompass the many-sided interests and abilities that are shown, and at the same time to overcome the personality traits shown by the

Moon-Uranus square. Mars is much too weakly placed to counteract this square by sheer drive, and Jupiter too weak to enable this individual to take a broad view of himself and his surroundings, to organize his resources, and to make sound judgments. In addition, Neptune in the eighth house ("escape from life") squares the Sun and Mercury in the fifth house, which will produce further complications in the personality. The situation may improve somewhat in the latter part of life as the majority of planets are in the western half of the horoscope. Finally, the position of so many planets below the horizon is not, generally speaking, an indication of prominence.

Example 2

Aries rising and the very strong position of Mars indicate considerable energy and activity, and the same is shown by the Sun, Jupiter, Venus, Mars, Saturn and Uranus in angular houses. The tenth house planets are by no means without bad aspects, but on the whole their position is quite favorable. The strong Capricorn influence shows unwavering ambition, tenacity, and a sharp sense of reality. Aries rising and the strong Mars indicate medicine or surgery, and Mars conjunct Mercury in the ninth house is an indication of scholarship in the field of medicine. The strong Jupiter shows clearly the joviality of this man as well as similar traits of character favorable for professional success.

This prominent physician was the thirteenth of twenty-five children whose father, a civil servant, did not have the means to provide his son with a higher education. While still in secondary school he was obliged to pay for his education by tutoring. After denying himself many things in order to complete his medical studies, he became a country doctor in a relatively short period of time. He then obtained the position of assistant in a special clinic, and not long after, he became a university lecturer. Still later he was made a professor there and his scholarship won for him a wide reputation both in Germany and abroad.

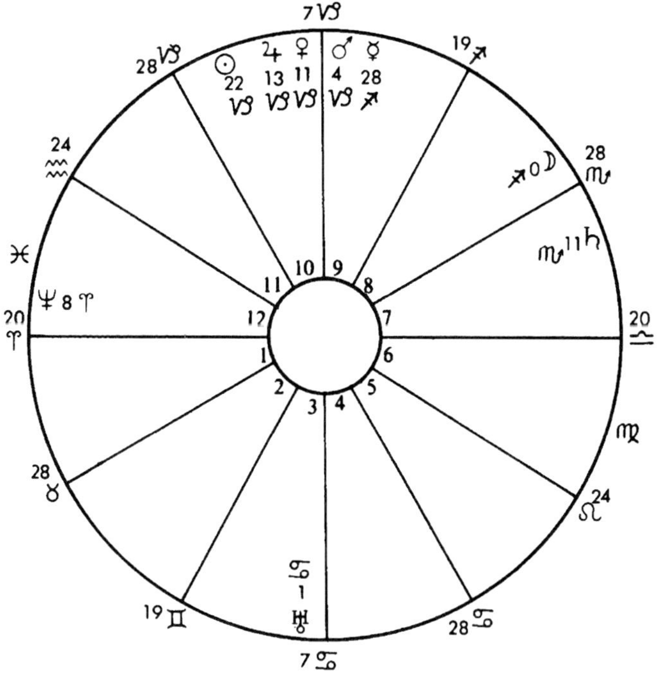

Example 2

This is a striking example of how little importance are background and environment when there is ability and strength of character.

Example 3

Aquarius rising, the dominant Mercury, and the third house emphasis all indicate a mental type of person who is capable of considerable intellectual development. Mercury, strongly placed in the mutable sign Gemini, shows many-sided interests accompanied by a strong desire for knowledge. The sextile of Mercury to Venus confers a feeling for beauty, and the sextile of Neptune to the Ascendant reveals a capacity for sympathetic understanding and an interest in psychology, mysticism and the occult. There is

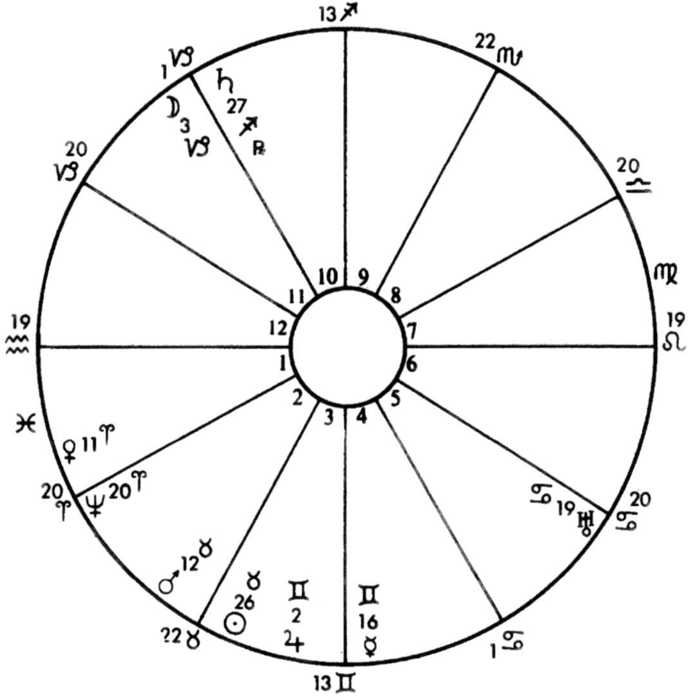

Example 3

little doubt that the horoscope shows literary talent, but it does not show the capacity to successfully combat the problems posed by an unfortunate environment. The energy factors of this horoscope are not strongly enough placed, and the conjunction of the Moon and Saturn in the most positive of the four quadrants will make it difficult for this individual to assert himself. The majority of planets below the horizon shows his inability to organize his life according to some plan, and this is shown by the lack of planets in the angular houses as well.

In this case, poor education and an unfavorable childhood environment were not conducive to the development of his innate abilities.

While still young, this man wanted to be a teacher—an ambition based on correct instincts—but poverty obliged him to go into the printing trade and he was unable to continue his education.

However, in this way the connection with literature was first brought about. His interest in psychology and occultism developed soon after. After discovering his particular talent in this area he became an excellent hypnotist and before the World War wrote a pamphlet on the subject that was widely read. He suffered a serious financial setback while in the service during the war, when during his absence, he placed undue reliance on the judgment of his partner. Later, it always seemed that his many conflicting interests and activities prevented his organizing some plan to regain financial security. The lack of a thorough education made it difficult to put to use his scattered knowledge and experience. Although he was never really able to get himself established again, he did become the central figure in a small group of persons interested in the occult, where he found opportunity to exercise his talents with some greater prospects of success. As far as he was concerned, his profession only provided the material support that gave him the opportunity to pursue his real interests.

If he had been born in different circumstances he would have been an excellent writer.

CPSIA information can be obtained
at www.ICGtesting.com
Printed in the USA
LVOW07s0535080217
523493LV00008B/206/P

9 780866 901666